Miniature Lamps of the Victorian Era

Marjorie Hulsebus

Schiffer Publishing Ltd.

4880 Lower Valley Road, Atglen, PA 19310 USA

Dedication

I would like to dedicate this book to my family and lamp collector friends who have been a constant source of support and especially to Yvonne Lynch for helping me in the final stages of preparation. Only a fellow lamp collector knows the passion that drives each one of us to constantly be looking for an addition to our ever growing collections.

A Note Regarding Color

The images in this book were contributed by many generous individuals. Because lighting conditions and camera equipment varied, there may be variations in color. The publisher has reproduced the photographs as accurately as possible, but where there are discrepancies, the description in the caption should be used.

Published by Schiffer Publishing Ltd.
4880 Lower Valley Road
Atglen, PA 19310
Phone: (610) 593-1777; Fax: (610) 593-2002
E-mail: Info@schifferbooks.com

For the largest selection of fine reference books on this and related subjects, please visit our web site at
www.schifferbooks.com
We are always looking for people to write books on new and related subjects. If you have an idea for a book please contact us at the above address.

This book may be purchased from the publisher.
Include $3.95 for shipping.
Please try your bookstore first.
You may write for a free catalog.

In Europe, Schiffer books are distributed by
Bushwood Books
6 Marksbury Ave.
Kew Gardens
Surrey TW9 4JF England
Phone: 44 (0) 20 8392-8585; Fax: 44 (0) 20 8392-9876
E-mail: info@bushwoodbooks.co.uk
Free postage in the U.K., Europe; air mail at cost.

Copyright © 2004 by Marjorie Hulsebus
Library of Congress Control Number: 2004105859

Designed by Mark David Bowyer
Type set in ZapfChan Bd BT/Dutch801 Rm BT

ISBN: 0-7643-2104-8
Printed in China
1 2 3 4

Acknowledgments

When I finished writing *Miniature Victorian Lamps* in 1996, I never imagined the number of unlisted lamps that would surface in such a short time. However, with the networking of the Night Light Club members and the popularity of the Internet, this has occurred. Friends and lamp collectors have encouraged me to assemble the lamps into another book. I have also been able to add new information about these old lamps.

Words can not express my appreciation to each and every one of the contributors listed below because this book would not have been possible without their tireless effort in providing the support and wealth of material I've amassed for the book contents. My gratitude to each and every one of you: Betty Barrett; Ralph and Angie Baumgardner; Barbara Bridges; Fran and Jack Carpenter; Carlton and Marion Cotting; Bob and Kathy Culver; Dr. M. Helena Etzel; Fostoria Glass Gallery; Sharon Fredrickson; Priscilla Goodger; Kathy and Paul Gresko; Rick Hornwood; Frank Keathley; Wayne King; Charlie and Jane Knox; Robert Lawrence; Pete and Yvonne Lynch; Frank and Karen McWright; Art Morell; Oldenlite II; Ray and Betty Plankinton; Hugh Pribell; Jean Privett; Bob and Pat Ruf; Kay and Barry Schwartz; Howard E. Smith; Gerry Turner; Jack Washka; Betty Lou Weicksel; Kris Williamson; Judy White; Mike Wood; Darrel Zbar.

My special thanks to Frank and Karen McWright for sharing their wealth of knowledge, for their patience with my endless questions and their unfailing support. I owe you a debt of gratitude. To my friend Gerry Turner, thank you for constantly helping me with computer problems, pushing me when I didn't feel I was worthy of the task of completing another book and your optimistic encouragement and help. To Fil Graff of *International Guild of Lamp Researchers* for images of European lamps and Yvonne Lynch for her helpful suggestions on the layout of the book and to Darrel Zbar for his wonderful synopsis of early European glass manufacturers. And last, but not least, I would like to express my deep appreciation to Bob and Pat Ruf for their tireless hours of photographing lamps from collections in California and Nevada. I am extremely grateful to you both for giving your time and energy on my behalf.

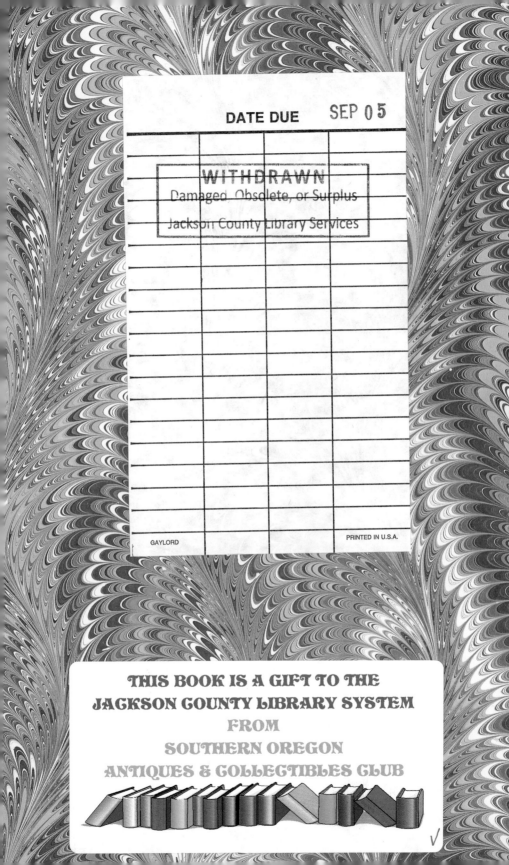

Contents

Introduction 6

Catalog Reprint of Firefly Lamps 9

Unlisted Lamps 10

Contemporary Lamps 237

Fluid Burning Related Items 239

Catalog Reprint of Foreign Burners 242

Catalog Reprints of European Lamps 243

A Brief History of European Miniature Lamps 245

Reproduction of Victorian Miniature Oil Lamps 254

Bibliography 256

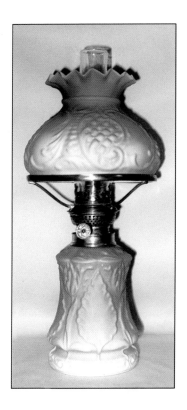

Introduction

Welcome to *Miniature Lamps of the Victorian Era.* The reference provides you with pictures and descriptions of nearly 600 beautiful miniature oil lamps that have not been pictured in previous books or are variations of lamps that have been published before but not documented until now. Most of these lamps were made in the late 1800s, often referred to as the "Victorian" era. To add to the perspective of understanding miniature oil lamps, estimated current values have also been provided for your information.

Regardless if you are an experienced miniature lamp collector, antique dealer, just beginning to collect lamps or glass, this book, along with other previously written books, will provide you a wealth of important information.

Background

So what would these little miniature oil lamps say if they could talk of their history? Dwellings were not large in size in the late 1800s, so miniature oil lamps were used as lighting for small bedrooms, hallways, and children's areas. Their larger counterparts were used in the dining and living areas of the dwelling. The more common clear glass utilitarian lamps with clear chimneys (and usually without shades) were sold by the dozen for around .95 cents. The fancier lamps with shades, decoration or embossing such as Smith 1-395 were also offered by the dozen for as much as $4.35. Miniature oil lamps were made from various types of glass. After understanding their popularity today and seeing the values of their worth, these little lamps would probably have a lot to say!

Markets and Values

Speaking of values... like any other antique or collectible, miniature oil lamps are subject to all the usual criteria – age, completeness or originality, condition, type of glass, scarcity, and desirability. Antiques and collectibles in general have always seemed to increase in value over the years and miniature oil lamps have followed this trend. Miniature oil lamps were typically sold in the standard antique publications, stores, flea markets, and estate auctions. Beginning in the middle 1990s with the popularity of the Internet and "on-line" auctions like eBay®, the market for miniature oil lamps changed remarkably. Although there have been price guides for miniature oil lamps published as recently as 1998 by this author, the "markets and values" now are world-wide and prices for lamps are somewhat determined daily as all types of bidder's pay Internet auction prices.

The price ranges stated in this book are based on the current market values at the time of this publication. Price ranges were determined by considering several sources including the lamps owner, other respected collectors, eBay®, on-line auctions, and estate auctions. The price ranges reflect lamps that are assumed to be in perfect condition, i.e. slight flakes and roughness excluded. Therefore, the price ranges are meant to be used as a guide. The prices listed in this book are not in any way warranted by the puplisher, author, or contributors.

Many of the lamps you see in this book would probably have not been known if it were not for the Internet. And, lastly, the popularity of miniature oil lamps is evidenced by the growing number of collectors and organizations, such as the Night Light Club, that have been formed around the common interests in miniature oil lamps.

Foreign vs. American

Advertising pictures and manufacturing diagrams from various American glass and oil lamp manufacturers have been reproduced in books previously published on miniature oil lamps. Lamps that were not manufactured in America were usually identified by the type of burners and were described as having a "foreign burner" unless the name of the burner manufacturer was molded into the round wick turner, i.e. Sparbrenner or Kosmos. The "collars" (round part that is fixed to the lamp base into which the burner screws) of these foreign lamps were also different in styling, and varied in diameter and threading. American burners, therefore, would not screw into the foreign collars and visa versa. Other differences between American and foreign made miniature oil lamps included the diameters and styling of the clear glass chimneys. A catalog copy of various foreign burners can be found on page 242.

Finally, but not surprisingly, there seems to be some differences in the styling of lamps with shades. The glass, color, patterns, and designs of the shade and base usually matched in American made lamps. Although this is also true of the foreign lamps, the foreign lamps seemed to vary more. For example, it was not uncommon for a foreign lamp to have a translucent base with a frosted shade. Foreign lamps were made during the 1800s in Sweden, Germany, Denmark, and some other parts of Europe. Please see the article at the back of this book entitled "A Brief History of European Miniature Oil Lamps" written by Darrel Zbar.

Figural Lamps

What this book refers to as "figural lamps" is common nomenclature associated with other books and miniature oil lamps collectors. The bases of figural lamps are in shapes ranging from a log cabin to a shoe; from a cherub to an animal; a court jester to a Dutch girl. There are both American and foreign made figural lamps. Although some figural lamps have matching shades or shades that have some similarity to the base, such as Smith 1-493 or 497, it seems more common that a figural may NOT have a shade or the shade is a plain utilitarian-type shade. In a few very rare miniature figural lamps the burner and chimney were hidden by the shade, which along with the base, made up the figure. Examples of this are found in the Skeleton (Smith I-490), Nippon owl (Smith I-495), and Capo de Monte owl (Hulsebus I-276), and porcelain elf (Hulsebus II-249).

Reproductions

Miniature oil lamps have been "reproduced" since around the 1940s. Because of the increasing desirability for miniature oil lamps (and patents have expired!) and world-wide Internet marketing and technology, reproductions of miniature oil lamps is becoming more popular. In fact, with the use of laser technology and computers, miniature oil lamps may be reproduced with precise definition making it even harder to distinguish from original lamps. As any "buyer should be aware," miniature oil lamp buyers are encouraged to do their research before purchasing a lamp.

There are numerous pictures of reproduction lamps made by B&P Lamp Supply Inc. in the back of this book but even with research, you can make a mistake. It is called, "paying for your education."

I have always encouraged collectors to share information and knowledge. What you know is precious and needs to be passed on. Network and join collector clubs such as the Night Light organization. The more we share, the more enjoyable the adventure. Happy Lamping!

Catalog Reprint of Firefly Lamps

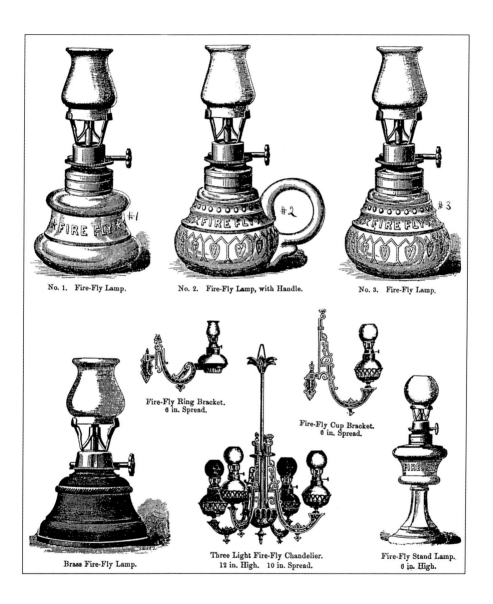

No. 1. Fire-Fly Lamp.

No. 2. Fire-Fly Lamp, with Handle.

No. 3. Fire-Fly Lamp.

Fire-Fly Ring Bracket.
6 in. Spread.

Fire-Fly Cup Bracket.
6 in. Spread.

Brass Fire-Fly Lamp.

Three Light Fire-Fly Chandelier.
12 in. High.   10 in. Spread.

Fire-Fly Stand Lamp.
6 in. High.

Unlisted Lamps

1. Small clear glass lamp embossed "Matchless" with stars on the font. No burner shown. 2.3". *Washka collection.* $75+.

2. Small bottle lamp with cork burner and string wick. Embossed "THE LITTLE GEM" on one side and "NIGHT LAMP" on the reverse. 3.6". *Culver collection.* $75+.

3. Small bottle lamp with cork burner and string wick. Embossed "THE EUREKA" on one side and "W. WHITE & SON SE LONDON" on the reverse. 3.6". *Culver collection.* $75+.

4. Small clear pear shaped alcohol lamp with drop-in cork burner. Melon Ribbed. 3". *Author's collection.* $75+.

5. Small bottle green colored glass with ribbing. Embossed "THE LAMP" on face and "C H & S" on the reverse. Glass is thick and filled with bubbles. Cork burner and string wick. 3.5". *Culver collection.* $75+.

6. Pressed clear glass lamp with brass camphene burner; 2.5" to top of collar. *Privett collection.* $100+.

7. Small light green base with "Ditmar" embossed on the middle band of the base. Also embossed on the base in smaller letters, "Fabrique en Allemagne" and "Made in Germany." Chimney may or may not be original. Ditmar marked burner. 6". *Howard Smith collection.* $125+.

8. Clear finger lamp marked "CHIQUITIN" on front and "PATENTADO" on the reverse. The burner is made of hard molded substance, also marked with the same words on the neck of the burner. 6.4". *Culver collection.* $125+.

9. "The Little Banner." 4.5". Original 1877 offering by P&A. *McWright collection.* $75+.

11. Cobalt blue glass font with white milk glass shade. Embossed on bottom of lamp is, "1877 PAT APP FOR." Chinook burner. 4.5". *Knox collection.* $200+.

10. Crystal font with white milk glass shade. Side of font is embossed "Little Lula's Night Lamp." Olmsted style burner. 3.5". *Knox collection.* $150+.

14. Small clear finger lamp embossed "TAKAHASHI" and five embossed stars across the back. No burner shown. 2". *Gresko collection* $75+.

12. Clear Glass embossed "Little Beauty." White milk glass shade. Olmsted burner. 3.75". *Author's collection.* $150+.

13. *Left:* Sun-purpled, crystal lamp with applied handle. Bottom signed "THE UNION LAMP CO." Chimneyless burner signed "THE UNION LAMP CO. BRIDGEPORT CT." Thumbwheel signed "October 20 '68." 4". *McWright collection.* $250+. *Center:* Crystal lamp embossed "UNION" on its side. One piece Chinook burner and collar. WMG chimney shade. 3.87". *McWright collection.* $250+. *Right:* Crystal lamp with applied handle. Side embossed "UNION PATENT APL 24 '77." WMG chimney shade. 3.75". *McWright collection.* $250+.

15. Crystal finger lamp with embossed ribs and "The Little Favorite" around the shoulder of lamp. White milk glass shade. Olmsted style burner. 4.5". *Knox collection.* $250+.

16. Frosted font with applied glass handle. Embossed "Moonlight." Acorn burner. 2.18". *McWright collection.* $150+.

17. Amber finger lamp embossed "The New York" on one side and "E.R.& Co." on the reverse side. 2.7" to top of the collar. Acorn burner. Also found in blue. *Carpenter collection.* $135+.

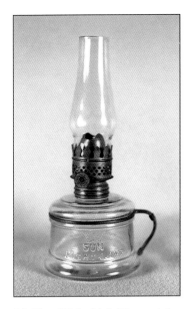

18. Cobalt blue finger lamp with an applied highly arched handle. Tapered font. Collar dated 1875/76. Acorn burner. 2.78". *McWright collection*. $175+.

20. "Sun Night Light" in crystal glass. Same metal handle as found on Smith I-29. Nutmeg burner. 2.5". *McWright collection*. $125+.

19. White milk glass finger lamp with embossed fleur-de-lis style pattern. Flattened wire band and handle. Nutmeg burner. 2.5". Knox collection. $125+.

21. Clear finger lamp with applied handle; one large embossed star opposite handle. Hornet burner. 2.75". *Ruf collection*. $85+.

24. Clear glass ribbed finger lamp with applied handle with small flip. Spring loaded collar dated "July 24 77." 1.75". *Author's collection.* $75+.

22. Virginia Night Lamp as pictured in *Our Drummer* catalog, Butler Brothers, New York, February 1900 issue and shown in Smith II on page 11. This lamp is different from the lamp pictured in Smith Book I-53 in that this one has a molded and threaded hole in the bottom which screws onto the tin saucer base. The saucer is 5" in diameter and has a crown and PATENTED embossed on the underside. 3.1" tall. *Culver collection.* $175+.

23. Clear glass finger lamp with paneling and clear applied handle. Burner marked "Made in Poland." 3.5". *Author's collection.* $75+.

26. Teal blue paneled reflector lamp. Unmarked foreign burner. 2.5" to the top of the collar. *Author's collection.* $125+.

25. Cobalt finger lamp with applied handle. One piece collar and alcohol burner with threads that screw onto base neck. 2.5" to the top of the collar. *Author's collection.* $125+.

27. Custard glass finger lamp with purple and red flowers, green leaves, and a blue band on the top and bottom. Nutmeg burner. 2.5". *Gresko collection.* $175+.

28. Silver plated finger lamp with shell decorations. Marked on the bottom "James W. Tufts Boston Warranted Quadruple Plate." 7.1". *Howard Smith collection.* $100+.

29. Small blue finger lamp. Glass has slight panel design. White milk glass shade on small foreign burner. 5". *Author's collection.* $175+.

31. Pink opaline finger lamp with applied white opaline handle. Burner marked "Wright & Butler." White milk glass shade. 5". *Author's collection.* $350+.

30. Green glass with white enameled floral décor. Olmsted burner and white milk glass chimney. 3.75". *McWright collection.* $175+.

32. Dark blue glass finger lamp. Foreign Nutmeg burner. 2.75". *Cotting Collection.* $125+.

33. Aqua milk glass finger lamp. Foreign burner. 2.5" to collar top. *Author's collection.* $85+.

35. The "Mei Foo" lamp produced by Standard Oil Co. of New York (Socony) in China to be given away to promote the use of their kerosene. "Mei Foo" ideograph appearing in the shield means "beautiful companion." Similar to the "Sterling" Smith II-131. Burner O size. *Photo courtesy of Fil Graff.* $50+.

34. Embossed brass saucer lamp with finger ring. 1.75" to the top of font; 6.5" to top of chimney. *Schwartz collection.* $75+.

36. Amber finger lamp with criss-cross pattern and hobnail embossed. Ribbed pedestal base. Vienna burner. 4". *Author's collection*. $100+.

37. Medium blue footed finger lamp with enameled floral décor. Acorn burner. 3.25". *Knox collection*. $175+.

38. Clear glass finger lamp in the form of a cottage with embossed lettering "Dietz & Co. London;" reverse side embossed "The Cottage Lamp." Burner marked "Dietz & Co. London." 2 7/8" to top of collar. *Pribell collection.* $600+.

39. Opaque green milk glass finger lamp, melon ribbed with embossed flowers separating panels. Hornet burner. 3.125". *Author's collection.* $75+.

40. Amethyst finger lamp with applied handle. Hornet burner. 3.5" to the top of the collar. *Ruf collection.* $150+.

41. Blue finger lamp with applied handle. Peacock eye embossed design attributed to Westmoreland Glass Co. Nutmeg burner. 3". *Fredrickson Collection.* $175+.

43. Peanut footed finger lamp. Crystal 3-mold font on a blue stem and foot with handle. Acorn burner. 5.75". *McWright collection.* $225+.

42. Chevron embossed crystal font on a light blue base with finger hold. Acorn burner. 5.750". *Knox collection.* $225+.

44. Clear glass finger lamp with chimney globe shade. Clear applied handle has flip curled at the base. Acorn burner. 5.5". *Author's collection.* $100+.

45. Cobalt finger lamp with matching ball-type shade. Similar to Smith II-192. Sternbrenner burner. 7". *Turner collection.* $125+.

46. Clear finger lamp with ribbing in bottom portion of base. Gold flecks in base and shade badly worn. Foreign burner. 5.75". *Zbar collection.* $125+.

47. Clear finger lamp with oval shaped chimney globe shade. Foreign burner. 7". *Zbar collection.* $125+.

48. Ivory colored porcelain, "rope" handled lamp with castle relief decorated in gilt and light blue. White porcelain candle-type screw in burner. Attached cap and chain. Foreign burner. 4.75" to the top of collar; 7" to the top of the burner. *Ruf collection.* $225+.

49. Pink and white opaline glass. Pink tank and font with white base bottom and white applied handle. Tip-top burner with screw holding clear chimney marked "ALCIUM FLINT." 3.75". *Turner collection.* $250+.

50. Cranberry swirl pattern font with two clear glass applied handles. English made Hornet-type burner. Known as a "pass lamp." 4" to top of the collar. *Turner collection.* $225+.

51. Queen's Necklace pattern lamp in crystal glass. Nutmeg burner. Molded handle. 7.25". *McWright collection.* $650+.

52. Emerald green glass with optic diamond paneling on base and shade. Foreign burner. Applied handle. 6.5". *McWright collection.* $400+.

53. Blue clambroth finger lamp with satinized shade. Similar to Smith I-181. Foreign burner. 5.25". *Author's collection.* $400+.

54. Light blue stem lamp with optic paneled font and rounded top. Embossed notching on edge of shoulder. Manhattan burner. 6" to collar-top. *McWright collection.* $175+.

55. Riverside beaded bands pattern in crystal. Nutmeg burner. 6.5". *McWright collection*. $200+.

57. Two part stem lamp made of flint glass. Font has ten panels; six on the base. 5". *Culver collection*. $125+.

56. Clear stem lamp. Embossed font with rings of beads above and below the design. Paneled stem. Wrong burner. 6.125" to the top of the collar. *Ruf collection*. $100+.

58. Clear stem lamp with spill lip around font. Six lines of beads down the stem to scalloped foot. Unmarked burner. 5.25" to the top of the collar. *Ruf collection.* $125+.

59. Paneled "Bulls-Eye" type stem lamp with concave bulls-eyes. 5.75" to the top of the collar. Possible whale oil lamp. *Ruf collection.* $100+.

60. Clear glass embossed stem lamp. Acorn burner. 5.5" to top of collar. *Cotting Collection.* $150+.

61. Clear glass stem lamp with fish scale base. Similar to Smith II-170 with plain font. Clinch style collar. 5.2". *Culver collection.* $125+.

63. Regal Fancy Panel lamp by Riverside Glass. Acorn burner. 5.375". *McWright collection.* $200+.

62. Miniature stem lamp in honey amber colored font with matching amber chimney. The font has fine line ribbing alternating with areas of iridized glass with a hollow formed stem. Nutmeg burner. 5.5". *Fredrickson Collection.* $125+.

64. Little Crown lamp. Cast metal gilded pedestal with a crystal ribbed font, circa 1877. Olmsted type burner with white milk glass chimney-shade. 3.75" to the collar-top. *McWright collection.* $350+.

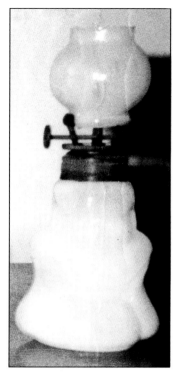

66. White opaline glass lamp in the shape of a Buddha. Original white opalescent shade. Olmsted type burner. Similar to Hulsebus I-59. 4.5". A*uthor's collection.* $175+.

65. Crystal stem lamp embossed "TRIUMPH" on font. Olmsted-type burner and white milk glass chimney shade. 6.5". *McWright collection.* $225+.

67. White milk glass lamp embossed "Firefly" and six stars. White milk glass ball shade as shown in original catalog by F.H. Lovell & Co. 1877-78 found in the front of this book. See Smith I-9. Olmsted burner. 5.5". *Author's collection.* $300+.

69. White opaline pedestal type lamp with matching shade. Traces of red and gold décor. Olmsted type burner. Similar to Hulsebus I-59. 4.75". *Author's collection.* $175+.

68. Clear glass lamp with flowers and leaves embossed on the font. Crinkle embossing on the stem. White milk glass ball shade. Olmsted burner. 6.5". *Author's collection.* $200+.

71. Cranberry glass with mercury lining and white "window" pattern. Similar to Smith I-522. Nutmeg burner. 6" to top of burner. *Turner collection.* $300+.

70. Cranberry opalescent coin dot font on a brass base. Font lined with mercury. Thought to be original as is. Nutmeg burner. 5". *McWright collection.* $300+.

72. White Milk glass lamp with embossed vine scrolling. Also found in other colors and glass. 3". Nutmeg burner. *Cotting collection.* $75+.

74. Blue translucent ribbed pattern font with white milk glass ribbed shade that fits over a clear chimney. Olmsted-type burner. 6.25". *Turner collection.* $275+.

73. Pale green milk glass base in ornate brass holder. Burner thumbwheel marked "Ditmar Brunner A.G." 2.5" to top of collar. *Privett collection.* $125+.

75. Green translucent glass glow-type lamp with decorative base and matching top. Glass glow-type burner. 5". *Turner collection.* $175+.

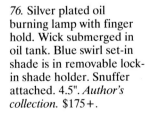

77. Clear glass base with copper tank. Wick turner and hinged snuffing cap. Used to put sealing wax on envelopes. 3". *Turner collection.* $75+.

76. Silver plated oil burning lamp with finger hold. Wick submerged in oil tank. Blue swirl set-in shade is in removable lock-in shade holder. Snuffer attached. 4.5". *Author's collection.* $175+.

78. Copper base with brass bottom and brass "skirt" around the burner. Cobalt blue shade. "Made in Sweden" marked on bottom. 5.5". *Turner collection.* $125+.

80. Clear glass beehive base and red painted clear glass shade with heart design. Screw-on type foreign burner. 4.25". *Turner collection.* $50+.

79. Blue translucent glass lamp with oval shaped chimney globe shade. Foreign burner. 7". *Zbar collection.* $175+.

81. Two types of clear glass pedestal lamps. Both have flashed red swirled shades. One has red flashed font. Also found with no flashing. Burner marked "Konishi Japan." 5.25". *Author's collection.* $35 ea.

82. Small metal filigree base painted black. Original white milk glass shade rests on attached shade ring holder. Burner marked "Night Light." 6". *Author's collection.* $225+.

83. Turquoise translucent glass base with painted floral design and gold painted trim. Milk glass shade painted with floral design. Collar marked "Pat'd Apr 13, 1876 March 21, 1876." Similar to Hulsebus I-9. Olmsted burner. 5.5". *Turner collection.* $200+.

84. Purple milk glass painted with white flowers. Olmstead type burner. Similar to Hulsebus I-8. 5". *Author's collection.* $175+.

85. Pink opaline lamp with gold tracery banding. Body of lamp has fired on finely detailed spray of wildflowers. Olmstead burner. White milk glass shade may or may not be original. 5". *Fredrickson Collection.* $225. With correct shade $300+.

86. White milk glass base painted brown to resemble a basket. White milk glass shade. Foreign burner. 6". *Author's collection.* $100+.

87. White milk glass lamp with basket weave design on shade and base. This is the correct version of Smith I-277. Acorn burner. 6.5". *Author's collection.* $250+.

88. White milk glass lamp with gold trim paint. Screw-on collar. Nutmeg burner. 6.5". *Oldenlite II collection.* $100+.

89. Satinized milk glass with rust colored vine-like décor. "Will-O'-the-Wisp" night lamp as pictured in the Smith-Brodewold Glass Company of Pittsburgh advertisement in *China, Glass and Lamps,* August 17, 1892, as noted in Ann McDonald's *Evolution of the Night Lamp.* 7.9". *Culver collection.* $225+.

90. Blue milk glass lamp with embossed flowers on the base; smooth chimney globe shade. See Smith II-85. Acorn burner. 6.5". *Author's collection.* $175+.

91. Blue milk glass base and shade. Similar to Hulsebus I-30 but without vertical flutes on base. Foreign burner. 5.5". *Cotting Collection.* $350+.

92. Blue milk glass with embossed ribbing and design on base with ribbed swirl shade. Similar to Smith II-396 with different shade. Collar marked JKA*DRGM. Foreign burner. 7.5". *Culver collection.* $325+.

93. Midnight blue translucent lamp similar to Hulsebus I-124. Foreign burner. 5". *Author's collection.* $225+.

94. Amber lamp with "looping" design in the base. One piece tin collar/burner which slips over neck of the base. Unmarked burner. 5.5". *Author's collection.* $200+.

95. Emerald green lamp similar to Hulsebus I-123. Slight paneling in shade. Burner marked "Ditmar Australia." 6". *Author's collection.* $200+.

96. Amber glass lamp. Foreign burner. 5.25" to the top of the shade which may or may not be original. *Ruf collection.* $75+.

97. Clear glass lamp similar to Smith I-229 with embossed flowers and "netted" background. Also found in other colors. Acorn burner. 6.25". *Author's collection.* $125+.

99. Green clear six-sided base with embossed design. Acid etched ball shade. Sternbrenner burner. 6.5". *Turner collection.* $150+.

98. Clear glass embossed lamp. Base is satinized; shade is not. 6.75". *Reesebeck collection*. $250+.

100. Gold-wash footed base with clear shade painted with a house and flower scene. Acorn burner. 6.75". *Barrett collection.* $275+.

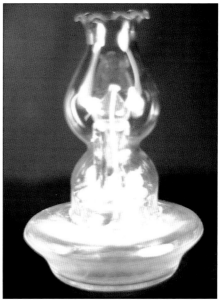

102. Clear glass base with glass burner and tooled glass chimney shade. Base signed "Firebug Pat app'd for." 5.75" high, 3.5" wide. *McWright collection*. $225+.

101. Cranberry and white spatter base with embossed ribbing. Clear ribbing on chimney globe shade. Acorn burner. 6.5". *Lynch collection*. $250+.

103. Tray based lamp with font assembly on a swivel to allow for carrying. The brass handled base has a center piece of stone or marble to give it some weight. Font is yellow or Vaseline glass. Foreign burner. 7.8". *Washka collection*. $250+.

104. Skater's lantern. Holmes, Booth & Hayden brass lantern with signed globe. Patent dated Feb 6ᵗʰ 1877. Thumbwheel signed "Holmes, Booth & Hayden Waterbury Ct.". 10". *McWright collection.* $450+.

105. Gimbaled lamp with brass base; porcelain font has blue, gold and red décor. Lamp has both finger ring and hanging ring. Possibly French in origin. Width of base is 5". Height when standing to top of collar is 4.5". *Schwartz collection.* $175+.

106. Miniature brass miner's lamp. Presentation piece signed Karl Lohr with crossed sledges and wedges. Base signed GEDIDONIT. Not old—probably contemporary. 6.125". *McWright collection.* $30+.

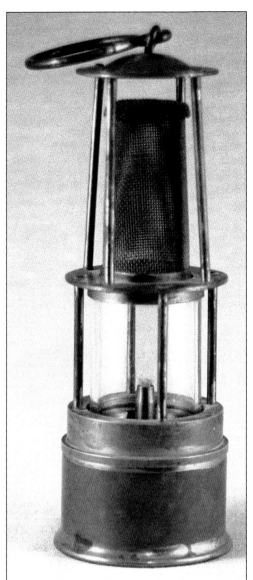

107. Miniature brass miner's lamp; 6.5" to top of lamp. *Privett collection*. $200+.

108. Brass skaters lantern with round ribbed handle. Cone dated "Pat'd Dec. 24th 1867 Holmes, Booth & Hayden Waterbury Conn." 8". *Lynch collection*. $300+.

110. Small brass traveling lamp with adjustable wick riser and chimney. Brass hinged lid. Unmarked burner. 4". *Author's collection.* $125+.

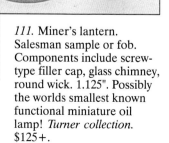

111. Miner's lantern. Salesman sample or fob. Components include screw-type filler cap, glass chimney, round wick. 1.125". Possibly the worlds smallest known functional miniature oil lamp! *Turner collection.* $125+.

109. Small brass lantern marked "OWL" by holes punched at the top. The burner and font can be removed for easy lighting and filling. Burner also marked "OWL." 7.3". *Washka collection.* $300+.

112. Brass tray lamp with reversed painted cream and gold glass font. Hammered shade and tray on applied feet. Nutmeg burner. Similar to Smith II-314. 8.5". *Baumgardner collection*. $175+.

114. Medicine clock with white milk glass dome and tin indicator. Separate drop in oil canister with attached burner. When lit, dome light was visible in the dark. Stamped on bottom "The Standard Novelty Co. Pat. Apr 6, 1866 New York." Clock winder key marked "Ansonia Clock Co." Pot metal base with screw on finger holder. 6.25". *Author's collection*. $500+.

113. Heavy iron finger lamp with dark rich patina. Inscribed "Wells unbreakable house lamp Patent" on one side and "safety from explosion A.C. Well & Co." on the other side. Also has a deeply carved tree design and fancy finger handle. 2.75". *Hornwood collection*. $150+.

115. White milk glass clock face embossed with an old fashioned sun. Brass spring wind mechanism. Removable clock is attached to a cast iron finger lamp, which receives a small clear font lamp with a green beehive shade. Time lamp burner. 7". *Gresko collection.* $1,000+.

116. Brass and clear glass lamp with ceramic shade to direct the light. 2.5" to top of collar. 8.75" from base to top of rod. Foreign burner. *Privett collection.* $125+.

117. "Bockett Microscope Lamp, Collins, London" inscribed around base. Nutmeg burner. Adjustable lens. 4" from font base to top of collar. *Ruf collection.* $450+.

118. Brass cigar lighter with cutter. Font is clear glass with incised close cross hatching. String wick with chain held wick cap. 4.75". *Cotting Collection.* $275+.

119. European-made brass double student lamp with green diamond patterned shades. Foreign burners. 12.5" high to top of center standard; 11.5" high to top of shades. *Oldenlite II collection.* $800+.

120. Brass student lamp with large acorn-shaped tank. Floral decorated white milk glass shade. Nutmeg burner. 11.75". *McWright collection.* $800+.

121. Metal street-type lantern with green paneled glass. Small font with unmarked burner. The number "37" and unknown stamp on bottom along with "1184/2," "t/y," and "4/11" scratched on bottom. 11.5". *Turner collection.* $75+.

122. Wall bracket lamp. Steel bracket painted brass and arm riveted to 2.75" tall wall plate. Arm is 5.5" long. Clear glass font with Vienna burner. *Cotting collection.* $125+.

123. Cranberry hanging float or candle lamp with banded brass canopy cover and matching undercover support. 6" from the top of the canopy to bottom of the support. *Fredrickson collection.* 275+.

124. Miniature hanging hall lamp with three spool canopy holding an open filigree meshwork body. Body is faceted with multi-colored jewels; original tin font is removable for lighting. Body of the lamp is 6.5". *Fredrickson Collection.* $275+.

126. Single brass float lamp. Curved branch supporting a cup where a float-type candle was placed. 8". Author's collection. $125+.

125. Float Lamp with silver pedestal ornate base and peg clear glass. Base marked "Rogers & Bros. Triple Plated." Referred to as the "Birthday Float Lamp." 7.25". Author's collection. $150+.

127. Float lamp. Cranberry glass with decorative brass stand. Similar to Smith II-32. 8". *Turner collection.* $200+.

128. Float lamp. Blue glass with pewter floral design stand. Similar to Smith II-32. 8". *Turner collection.* $175+.

129. Miniature Hanging Lamp. The font is attached to the metal yoke which is attached to the shade holder ring by tiny nuts and decorated bolts. Round amber "jewels" are inserted from the interior and held in place by metal tabs formed from the "punch work" openings in the shade. White milk glass chimney. Foreign burner. Top ring surrounds a metal smoke bell. 4.25" to top of shade. 9.5" to top of complete lamp. *Ruf collection.* $775+.

130. Hanging lamp, white milk glass shade with embossed design. "Night Lamp" burner. Lamp is 4.5" overall length is 8". *Turner collection.* $300+.

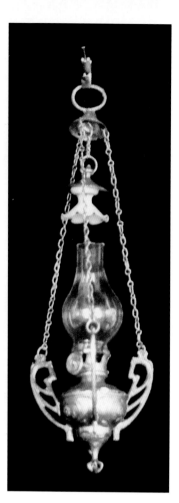

131. Hanging gilded metal lamp. 6.5" to top of ring, milk glass smoke bell, foreign burner. Possible doll house lamp. *Baumgardner collection.* $400+.

132. Kerosene/candle miniature parlor/library type hanging lamp. Cast brass arms hold six miniature candelabras. Cast chaining counterbalance type weighted pull down top canopy unit. Bristol shade with matching milk glass chimney is complimentary to the white candles. Miniature smoke bell. 17" from top of canopy to bottom of finial. Kosmos Brenner burner. *Fredrickson collection.* $800+.

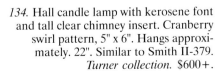

133. Brass hanging lamp with seahorses. The font and burner are brass with a very heavy patina. The inscribed plate reads "BUCKINGHAM SWOPE & CO BALTMORE, MD." The thinly soldered font is easily removed from the outside holder for filling and lighting. The wall bracket was added. Beehive shade. Overall height 14.75"; the diameter of the font is 5.75". *Hornwood collection.* $250+.

134. Hall candle lamp with kerosene font and tall clear chimney insert. Cranberry swirl pattern, 5" x 6". Hangs approximately. 22". Similar to Smith II-379. *Turner collection.* $600+.

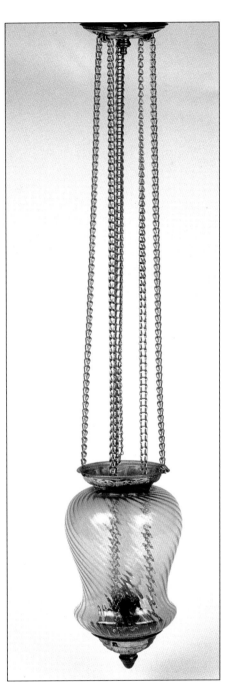

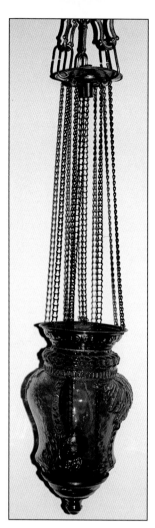

135. Hanging hall lamp with embossed cranberry globe. The globe itself is 6.5". The brass bottom pulls down on chains to reveal a font, burner, and chimney. 8.75" from top of brass to pull down knob. *Schwartz collection.* $600+.

136. Miniature hall hanging lamp; brass fixtures; embossed cranberry frosted and etched shade with six panels each depicting a cherub and flowers; shade is signed Eserco. 20" overall length; 6" shade. *Wood collection.* $600+.

137. Bracket lamp with tapered lamp font embossed "Brilliant" set in flower-form holder with grapevine arm. Unmarked burner. 2.125" to top of the collar. 6.75" to the top of the shade. *Ruf collection.* $700+.

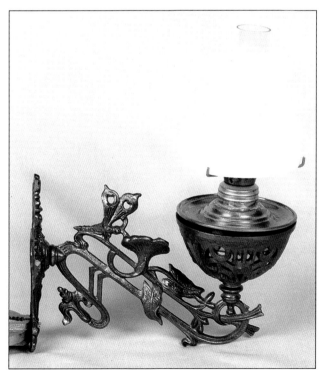

138. Bracket lamp with brass font and white milk glass shade set in cast iron scroll bracket. Acorn burner. 8.5". *Author's collection.* $275+.

139. Miniature wall bracket lamp. Cast iron with original gold gilt paint; cast open work arm shaped to resemble a trumpet vine and hummingbird motif. Original foreign burner and shade holder with milk glass font and matching Bristol stylized shade. The bracket which holds the lamp is 6" from the back plate to the font holder cup. *Fredrickson Collection.* $625+.

140. Gold gilded bracket lamp; white milk glass font with gold rings around the milk glass shade. Lamp is 7.5" to top of shade. Bracket is 3.5" tall; 6" wide. *Baumgardner collection.* $500+. ***a***

141. Wall-sconce lamp with green glass ball shade and matching font. Heavily embossed brass reflector with perforated brass and tin holder. Foreign burner. 7". *McWright collection*. $400+.

142. Bracket lamp with cranberry inverted thumbprint font and shade. Metal bracket with leaves and snail painted black. Foreign burner. 8". *Author's collection*. $700+.

143. Bracket lamp with cranberry font and shade in honeycomb pattern. Ornate cast iron bracket has flowers and leaves similar to Smith II-374. Foreign burner. 8.25". *Author's collection*. $700+.

144. Pair of green glass peg lamps with matching shades. Frosted bands on shades and fonts. Pink, white, and green enameled floral décor. Foreign burners signed "BEC ROND PARISIEN JR." Double wall-mounted bracket signed "E. MULLER PARIS." The height from bottom of arm to shade top is 10.75", from bottom of font to shade top is 7.5". *McWright collection.* $1,000+.

145. Piano lamps – matched pair of cranberry glass acid etched busts of music composers "Jos. Haydn, Mozart, Beethoven, J. Seb. Bach." Bohemian crystal tanks with indented pattern. Clear glass chimneys marked "J. B. Worre, 21. Frederiksborggade 21, KJ0BENHAVN. K. B0HMISK 8." Kosmos Brenner burners. Decorative iron brackets. 9". Similar to Fig. 439/440 in *Lampor och Lampartijlar* by Arvid Böhlmarks, Stockholm, Sweden 1887-1889. *Turner collection.* Price unavailable.

146. Brass pedestal lamp with embossing on shade and base. Blue jewels embedded in the shade. A separate vertical brass piece supports the shade ring. Foreign burner. 8". *Author's collection.* $150+.

147. Brass pedestal lamp with hammered design in shade and base. Green fringe of beading on the shade. Separate vertical brass piece supports the shade. Decorative overshot chimney may or may not be original to the lamp. Unmarked burner. 8.5". *Author's collection.* $150+.

148. Unassembled.

149. Brass lamp with design in shade and base. Shade is jeweled and fringed and rests on a rounded top chimney. Foreign burner. 10". *Authors collection.* $200+.

150. Jeweled brass lamp with fringed shade, clear glass globe shaped chimney. Similar to Smith Book 2-285,286 and 288. Foreign burner. 9.5". *Schwartz collection.* $200+.

151. Embossed brass lamp with jeweled and fringed shade. Unique tripod holds shade in place as shown in Hulsebus I-107. Unusual brackets attaching font to base. Cosmos Brenner burner. 12.5". *Schwartz collection.* $250+.

152. Candle stick peg lamp with ornate silver base depicting a coiled snake. The mouth of the snake holds candle stick base; end of tail is curled to form finger hold. Small circular opening for matches at the side of base. White Bristol shade. Twilight shade holder. Acorn burner. 12". *Author's collection.* $225+.

153. Column-style embossed metal base with drop-in font. 4.5" floral etched and frosted ball shade. Nutmeg burner. 14". *Knox collection.* $400+.

154. Multi-colored cloisonné base mounted on a round metal foot. Cobalt blue shade. Nutmeg burner. 9.125". *Oldenlite II collection.* $325+.

156. Silver plated base with four feet.
Scroll leaf handle. Removable oil font.
White milk glass shade with blue ground,
pink flowers, green leaves. Nutmeg
burner. 7.75". *Author's collection.* $150+.

155. Brass pedestal style decorated base
with incised yellow flower, green foliage
typical of Longwy Faience in the 1880s.
Yellow satin shade may not be original.
Nutmeg burner. 8.75". *Author's collection.*
$225+.

157. Red velvet with metal foot and embossed band, with insert metal canister. Wick riser worn but reads "B...... Co. P......, June......, Good Night." Shade hangs on chimney. 7.5". *Ruf collection.* $75+.

158. Brass base, decorative handles and cobalt blue ball shade. Clear glass tank font fits into brass base. Spar Brenner burner. 8.5". *Turner collection.* $175+.

160. Embossed brass base with Lithophane shade depicting "busts" of four different ladies. Acorn burner. 7.75" to top of the shade. *Ruf collection.* $350+.

159. Brass pedestal with lions head handles. White milk glass shade. Similar to Smith I-275. Foreign burner. 10". *Turner collection.* $175+.

161. Weighted brass base with Lithophane shade depicting four "lovers" scenes; stamped "116." Acorn burner. 7.75" to top of shade. *Ruf collection.* $350+.

162. Square engraved silver base with light blue optic shade. Base is marked "X" a decorated bugle, "Marlad, D, B & S, EPBM and NC1." "BE&S" on wick riser. 4.5" to top of collar, 9.75" to the top of shade. *Ruf collection.* $300+.

163. Metal base painted gray. Brass font. Green painted shade. Font embossed with angel heads and wings repeated three times. Foreign burner. 7.75". *Cotting Collection.* $275+.

164. B&H nickel plated brass hand lamp. Original fittings. Green cased 6" shade. 10.5". *McWright collection.* $200+.

166. Small blue Wedgwood lamp with a cameo on both sides; gold gilded stars and swirl design around the cameos. Bristol shade. Foreign burner. 3.75". *Baumgardner collection.* $125+.

165. Blue porcelain base with white castle relief in one of the concave panels. Foreign burner. White milk glass shade. 3.5" to top of collar, 6.25" to the top of the shade. *Ruf collection.* $225+.

167. Blue Wedgwood with angels on 2 sides; flower urns on opposite sides. White Bristol shade. Foreign burner. 7". *Author's collection.* $250+.

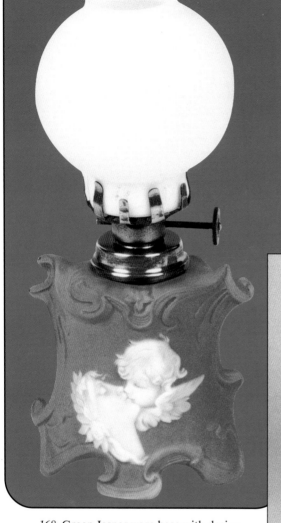

168. Green Jasper ware base with design in white relief of a lady kissing a baby. White satin glass shade. Base incised "3392." Foreign burner. 6.5". *Author's collection.* $325+.

169. Jasper ware lamp of a green stump shaped base and a white girl standing next to the stump. White Bristol-type embossed shade. Similar to Smith I-486. Foreign burner. 6.5". *Ruf collection.* $300+.

170. White milk glass base. Missing chimney globe shade in the shape of a cross. Referred to in Ann McDonald's book *Evolution of the Night Lamp* as the "Rock of Ages Night Lamp." 2.5" to the collar. *Author's collection.* $100+.

171. White porcelain lamp in the shape of a mandolin with cupid holding the bow. Gold highlighting scroll design. Acorn burner. 3.5". *Author's collection.* $225+.

172. Boy standing
beside a mandolin
shaped font. Nutmeg
type burner. 3.75". *Ruf
collection.* $225+.

173. White porcelain Dresden urn-type
base with colorful flowers, gold décor
and rose buds on font and lower footed
type base. Collar marked WELSBACH.
4". *Author's collection.* $135+.

175. White porcelain
smiling face with red dots
on collar and blue flowers
on the bow circling the
neck. Brass collar marked
"*DAISY* DRGM."
Vienna burner. 4".
Author's collection.
$225+.

174. Porcelain lamp with English
Nobleman's head peeking out of a wreath.
Fired on paint in blue and tan. Burner
marked "Welco English Make." Chimney
marked "Britray." Refer to Smith II-442.
9" to the top of chimney. *Author's
collection.* $375+.

177. Bisque pig in front of a tree trunk painted in shades of beige and brown. Embossed mark on bottom is "5707PS L 66." Hand painted is number "41." Hornet burner. 3.58". *Knox collection.* $225+.

176. Porcelain gondola in white, buff, and brown with gold highlights. Musician dressed in blue straddling the stern of the gondola. Foreign burner with white milk glass chimney. 3.5" to collar-top. *McWright collection.* $225+.

178. Bisque figural lamp of a boy with his pet dog and wagon. Pale pink and light blue décor with gold highlights. Nutmeg burner. 4" to top of collar. *Knox collection.* $250+.

179. White porcelain lamp depicting a girl with blue shoes and scarf sitting on a log with a cat painted in colors of tan and brown. Rust leaves and two rose buds applied to oval font. Numbers "6495" incised on base. Bristol decorated shade. Vienna burner. 6". *Author's collection.* $275+.

180. Porcelain walrus base in colors of green shading to white. White satin shade with green smudges is not original but compliments base. Foreign burner. 2.5" to the top of collar. *Author's collection.* $250+.

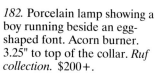

182. Porcelain lamp showing a boy running beside an egg-shaped font. Acorn burner. 3.25" to top of the collar. *Ruf collection.* $200+.

181. Figural lamp of a pig standing next to a blue bag. Pink satin shade. Foreign burner. Number "3" marked on the bottom of base. 7" to the top of shade. *Author's collection.* $225+.

183. Porcelain Victorian boy standing by a stylized font. Acorn burner. 3.75" to top of the collar. *Ruf collection.* $200+.

184. Porcelain girl dressed in blue with arms to her side. Impressed "2139" on lower back of figure. Foreign burner. 6.5" to top of the collar. *Ruf collection.* $200+.

186. Dragon in colors of tan with gold accents and tail forming a handle. Fancy blue spear stamped on bottom. Nutmeg burner. 2.75" to top of the burner. *Ruf collection.* $200+.

185. Porcelain girl dressed in pink with arms raised upward. Impressed "2137" on lower back of figure. Foreign burner. 6.5" to top of the collar. *Ruf collection.* $200+.

187. China house with windows on all four sides. Blue textured outline on house and gold highlighting windows and door. House chimney opening serves to hold clear cylindrical oil reservoir. Bottom incised "17." Acorn burner. 4.75". *Author's collection.* $325+.

188. Ceramic finger lamp with figure of girl with painted floral decorations and "Gute Nacht" in gilt script. Kosmos Rundbrenner burner. 9.5". *Privett collection.* $225+.

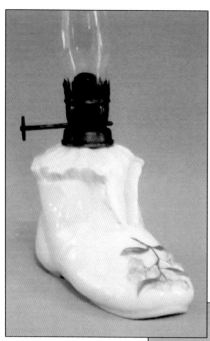

189. Porcelain boot
with blue flowers and
green leaves. "Lion
Lamp Works" burner.
3.5". *Baumgardner
collection.* $225+.

191. Pegged head with
painted eyes; possibly
Flemish. "Rd 27639"
on metal surrounding
porcelain peg which is
marked "Rd 27983."
3.5" to top of the collar
excluding the peg. *Ruf
collection.* $500+.

190. White porcelain
boot shaped lamp with
owl emerging from the
top. Owl has gold glass
eyes; buttons and laces
embossed on the boot.
Burner is marked
"Manufactured in
Germany F.T . Sale
Oxford Street." 6" to
top of collar. *Author's
collection.* $325+.

192. Porcelain peg lamp of a monkey face with brown glass eyes. Brass peg stamped "Rd 27639" and porcelain base of peg is embossed "Rd 23645." Kosmos Brenner burner. 3.5" from bottom of peg to the top of collar. *Ruf collection.* $500+.

193. Bisque lamp with boy sitting on a fence. Green, tan, brown, and yellow décor. Pink quilted ball shade. Foreign burner. 13". *Lynch collection.* $500+.

194. The heads of two children emerging from sides of a green stack. "PS" over "L" and "702" all stamped in blue on the base. "Feb'y 22 1877" on wick riser. 3.5". *Ruf collection.* $350+.

195. Porcelain lady in front of a green woven background wearing a hat, pink jacket, red boots, blue shorts. Base incised with "B704" in blue. Shade in colors of green, pink, and blue. Nutmeg burner. 7". *Author's collection.* $350+.

196. Porcelain base in green woven background with a white cat on one side; white dog on the other side. Base incised with " PS over "L" and 5701." Shade in colors of green, pink, and blue. Nutmeg burner. 7.25". *Author's collection.* $350+.

198. Gray green woven base with two figures protruding on opposite sides. Possibly they represent Sherlock Holmes and Watson. "5703" and "PSL" marked on base. Not original shade. 8". *Howard Smith collection.* $350+.

197. Girl holding a basket in front of green porcelain square basket weave mound. Base is stamped in blue "PS" over "L" and "5704." Foreign burner. 3.75" to the top of the collar. *Ruf collection.* $350+.

199. Bisque figural lamp with a square base with soft rust and light aqua blue background. Young girl and her pet cat peering out of a shuttered window on one side; young boy and his dog peering out of a shuttered window on the opposite side. Foreign burner. 5" high to top of collar; 8.5" high to top of shade pictured on lamp which is a newer red satin quilt embossed ball. *Knox collection.* $350+.

200. Porcelain figural of a full-figured blue decorated cherub standing in front of a large vase detailed in pale yellow. Lined wicker shade. Original foreign fittings switched to Acorn burner. 8". *McWright collection.* $400+.

201. White porcelain swan with slightly bent head. Heavy gold flower and leaf design on the egg that is resting on the birds' back and shoulders. Gold gilt on beak and webbed feet. 5" high to top of neck. Superior-Rund-Brenner burner. *Hornwood collection.* $400+.

202. White porcelain swan base with painted head. White milk glass ball shade. Sternbrenner burner. 6.25". *Turner collection.* $250+.

204. Barefoot blonde lady reclining on an oversized flower and artichoke stock. Lady dressed in a satin type shirt, holding a black hat. No markings. Foreign burner. 5.75" to top of collar. *Hornwood collection.* $300+.

203. Nude child with drape over front torso sitting on a log which rises to become a vase. The basket weave font is supported on gilded branches and stamped "Moore Bros." and "Rd 190756." The wick riser is marked "The Boudoir, E&M Co." 5.75" to top of the collar. *Ruf collection.* $325+.

205. White porcelain Goldfinch type bird sitting on twigs that are resting on the ground. Eyes, beak, claws, twig, and ground painted gold. Shade optional. Spar Brenner burner. 6.5" to top of collar. *Hornwood collection.* $450+.

206. Cherub leaning away from an elaborate shaped font with applied foliage and flowers. German mark stamped on bottom with "259" over a sideward "8" impressed. "E.T. Sale, Manufactured in Germany" burner. 5.5" to the top of collar. 13.5" to the top of pink cased shade. *Ruf collection.* $800+.

207. Porcelain girl dressed in green standing beside a stylized pink flower with buds. "4190" impressed on back near bottom. Foreign burner. 5.75" to top of collar. *Ruf collection.* $200+.

208. Wall mounted bisque figural of a smiling pudgy-cheeked character, possibly a cook. Foreign burner. 5.5" high x 4" deep x 3.25" wide. *Knox collection.* $300+.

209. Porcelain figural lamp. A boy standing beside an urn covered by a vine with leaves and fruits. White ground. Boy attired in knickers, blouse, bowed scarf, and cap. Pink, blue, yellow, green, and orange decor. No. "82" incised into foot. Floral decorated white milk glass shade. Foreign burner. 8.125". *McWright collection.* $400+.

210. Figural lamp of a boy and girl sitting in a bonnet. The bonnet sits on a brown frame similar to Smith I-485. Tiny gold dots outline the bonnet. Pink bow wrapped around the front. Found in various colors. Blue satin shade. Spar Brenner burner. 8". *Author's collection.* $650+.

212. Bisque angel lamp. Blue Bristol ball shade with blue and gold décor. Foreign burner. 5.5". *Lynch collection.* $400+.

211. Bisque cherub lamp with egg shaped font. White ball shade with blue, yellow, pink, and green décor. Spar Brenner burner. 9.5". *Lynch collection.* $450+.

214. Victorian boy standing beside
a flowered font. Impressed "4043"
on the bottom. Foreign burner. 6".
Ruf collection. $300+.

213. Bisque blooming rose with girl holding
goose in her lap. Tan, green, pink, and blue
décor. Frosted upturned ruffled shade with
white and gold painting. Foreign burner. 9".
Lynch collection. $450+.

215. Figural lamp of cream colored porcelain vase with tan and dark brown highlights. Sides decorated with embossed flowers, leaves, and stems in yellow, green and lavender. Figure of blonde girl to one side dressed in pink and blue trousers with lavender scarf. Base incised with "51." Pin cased shade. Spar Brenner burner. 8.5". *McWright collection*. $500+.

216. Bisque figural lamp. Pale yellow basket emerging from a blue Acanthus leaf clump growing on an earth tone foot. Full figure man, silver clad, with a half figure gnome talking in his ear. Gold pearls all-over. Pale yellow satin glass ball shade. Foreign burner. 8.125". *McWright collection*. $500+.

217. Porcelain base with figure of cupid off to one side. Medium pink décor with gold highlights. White milk glass 4.125" ball shade with transfer decoration of cupids. P&A Victor burner. 11.125". *Knox collection.* $450+.

219. Porcelain base with two applied figural cherubs trimmed in gold. Floral sprays baby blue color around edges. White Bristol shade. P/A Victor burner. 12".
Baumgardner collection. $450+.

218. Three small round open vases lamp. The bottom is marked "Royal Worcester England. C 31,45." Pink satin embossed shade optional. Foreign burner. 13" to top of the shade. *Ruf collection.* $850+.

220. Porcelain base of three cherubs a holding basket; similar to Smith II-333. Base is marked with crossed swords and "442" incised in the bottom. Milk glass shade with floral transfers and is marked Baccarat. Burner marked 'stern Bros. NY." 12". *Howard Smith collection.* $700+.

221. Porcelain lamp depicting an elephant head, trunk, and ears poking out of a crate. Green threaded glass upturned ruffled shade. Burner marked Eufsteck Brenner. 10". *Lynch collection.* $700+.

222. Swedish Majolica owl stamped "0" over undistinguishable trade mark and "CS" on bottom. Kosmos Brenner burner. 6.5" to top of collar. *Ruf collection.* $400+.

223. White porcelain dog with light brown glass eyes, blue collar, two raised front paws, and long tail wrapped around body. Impressions on base. 6.5" to the top of the collar. *Ruf collection.* $400+.

224. Gnome emerging from between antlers. The bottom is marked "6293" and "63." "Evered & Co. Ltd., London & Birm." on riser. 7.75" to top of the shade. *Ruf collection.* $800+.

225. Stork and child with book in front of pink egg-shaped font. Foreign burner. 7.75". R*uf collection.* $400+.

226. Porcelain owl with realistic glass eyes; feathers very detailed. Brown base and white Bristol shade. P&A Victor burner. 12.75". *Baumgardner collection*. $500+.

227. Porcelain owl in colors of tan and white. White Bristol shade. Base marked "William Whiteley China Manufactured in France." Also found in white. Kosmos Brenner burner. 13". *Author's collection*. $500+.

228. Porcelain base with three owls holding an oval shaped font with applied flowers. "Young's Nacht Light" on burner riser. Pink satin shade optional. 7.5" to the top of the collar. *Ruf collection.* $800+.

229. Three lions holding basket weave embossed font with applied flowers and foliage. German marked with "sitzendorf" and "56" on base. Kosmos Brenner burner. 6.5" to top of collar. *Ruf collection.* $400+.

231. Porcelain figure of a Dutch maiden carrying a Delft decorated vase. Milk glass ball shade. Spar Brenner burner. 10". *Baumgardner collection.* $250+.

230. Four elephant heads and front feet emerging from embossed font. Impressed "1090" over "2," written "250" over "VII," stamped "XY, 637, HP" inside wreath with bow. White milk glass decorated shade. Foreign burner. 6.5" to the top of the collar. *Ruf collection.* $800+.

233. Bisque figure of a young girl holding a bowl. A variation of Hulsebus I-238. Foreign burner. Acid etched shade with flower design added. 5.75" to top of the collar. *Hornwood collection.* $300+.

232. Bisque figure of a girl holding a watering can. White milk glass shade. Numbers "839" inscribed on bottom. Similar to Hulsebus I-238. Sternbrenner burner. 9". *Turner collection.* $200+.

234. Delft porcelain figural lamp depicting a young girl sitting beside a large covered basket. Typical blue delft décor of windmill scene. Back of the lamp is marked "Delft" and has the numbers "201+/15." Shade may or may not be original. Foreign burner. 6.25". *Williamson collection.* $400+.

235. Porcelain figural girl standing next to a large basket in colors of blue, white, and pink. Frosted upturned ruffled shade with painted décor. Foreign burner. 7.5". *Cotting Collection.* $400+.

236. Bisque boy standing beside a large vase. Raised flowers and leaves in shades of green and yellow. Lamp is similar to Hulsebus I-253. 9". *Schwartz collection.* $300+.

237. White metal Arab figural holding a reverse optic cobalt blue font with WMG shade. Foreign burner. 7" high to top of figural; 10.5" high to top of shade. *Knox collection.* $400+.

238. Full bodied parrot with red glass eyes. Pink milk glass conical shade. Base stamped "SP" over "1." Foreign burner. 6.75" to top of the collar, 11" to top of the shade. *Ruf collection.* $400+.

239. Three cherubs holding a porcelain font. Base signed **"William Whitely."** This lamp has large leaves and buds protruding from base. White Bristol shade. Similar to Smith II-333. Foreign burner. 13.25". *Baumgardner collection.* $600+.

240. Three cherubs holding up porcelain wicker weaved basket. Similar to Smith-II fig. 333. This lamp is slightly bigger. Also the cherubs are more detailed and their wings protrude outward. Foreign burner. 11.5". *Baumgardner collection.* $500+.

241. White porcelain begging shaggy dog in brown and white; brown glass eyes. Fired on paint with flesh colors around the eyes, tail, and base. Tan collar with gold highlights. Kosmos burner. 9.5" to top of collar. *Hornwood collection.* $625+.

243. Cast iron Ram lamp. Embossed brass burner and insert cover plate. Nailsea shade optional. Burner marked "Victor Co- PM MFG." Height 4.5" to top of the collar, 9.75" to top of the shade. *Hornwood collection.* $625+.

242. Squirrel sitting on a stump. Fired on paint in colors of light tan to darker fawn. Clay colored glass eyes. K&W burner. 8" to the top of the collar, 15" to the top of the cased umbrella shade. *Hornwood collection.* $800+.

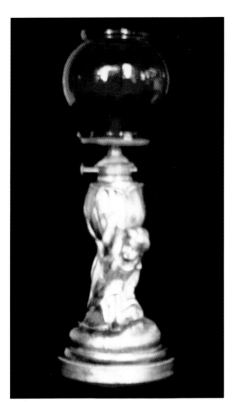

244. Pot-metal based lamp of a little girl supporting a tulip. Pet ratchet burner. Swirled pigeon blood shade. 9.5". B*aumgardner collection.* $300+.

245. Porcelain elephant lamp with colorful ivy décor on the base. Elephant ears are flattened; seal resting below his trunk. Kosmos Brenner burner. See Smith II 330 for similar lamp. Green painted shade. 5" to top of collar. *Author's collection.* $600+.

246. Porcelain swan lamp with small painted flowers on shade and base. Spar Brenner burner. 9.25". *Author's collection.* $600+.

247. Satinized Rubina glass lamp of a male bust purported to be that of Scottish poet Robert Burns on the base. Matching satinized Rubina glass shade in a swirling flame pattern. 10". *Howard Smith collection.* $900+.

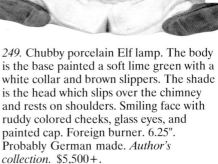

249. Chubby porcelain Elf lamp. The body is the base painted a soft lime green with a white collar and brown slippers. The shade is the head which slips over the chimney and rests on shoulders. Smiling face with ruddy colored cheeks, glass eyes, and painted cap. Foreign burner. 6.25". Probably German made. *Author's collection.* $5,500+.

248. Green milk glass lamp embossed "Columbus" on the bottom portion of the base. The reference in Smith-II, page 25 is a reprint of C.M. Livingston's *Silent Salesman* catalog dated 1894. It refers to this lamp as being "Decorated Bisque Finished Columbian Ware" and originally sold for $ .75 each or $4.72 per dozen. 8.75". Nutmeg burner. *Photo permission from Fostoria Glass Heritage Gallery.* $5,000+.

250. Unassembled.

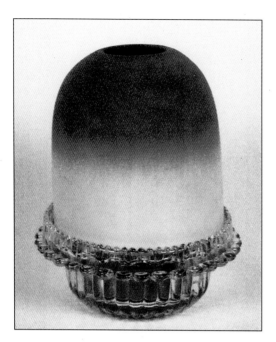

253. Blue embossed diamond fairy lamp style shade on a matching petal base. Clear glass font with burner signed "Chambers Patent." Lamp base signed "Rd 176239." Also found in Vaseline opalescent. 4.25". *McWright collection.* $550+.

251. Fairy-size Webb Burmese fairy lamp with clear lamp cup marked "Clarke Fairy Patent Trade Mark." The lamp cup holds a form fitting removable font with wick riser marked "Chamber Patent, Made in Germany." 5". *Ruf collection.* $550+.

252. Unassembled.

254. Northwood Leaf Mold pattern with dome shade and base. Satin-finished in light amber, cream, and pink. Nutmeg burner. 5.625". Sister lamp to Smith I-555. *McWright collection.* $2,000+.

255. Pink and white spatter glossy finish with gold flecks in dome shade and base. Northwood pattern as shown in Smith I-555. Nutmeg burner. 5.5". *Author's collection.* $2,000+.

256. Green milk glass lamp with decorated base and straight line chimney. Fired on painted flowers in yellow and orange, brown branches, and green leaves. Acorn burner. 6". *Author's collection.* $300+.

257. Blue porcelain lamp with embossed detail on shade and base. Scalloped shade top. Similar to Smith II-XLVII. Unmarked foreign burner. 6.75". *Author's collection.* $375+.

258. White milk glass with garland of pink and blue flowers, green leaves, and blue bands circle the shade and base. Nutmeg burner. 7.5". *Author's collection.* $225+.

259. White milk glass lamp with hand painted reddish flowers and green leaves. Acorn burner. 7.5". *Cotting Collection.* $225+.

260. White milk glass with highly embossed pattern of circles. Ribbing on top and bottom of shade and pedestal type base. Spar Brenner burner. 6.75". *Zbar collection.* $400+.

261. White opaline glass lamp with rust colored band on lower base. Spar Brenner burner. 9". *Barrett collection.* $225+.

262. White milk glass lamp shading from cream to deep rust. Spar Brenner burner. 8.5" *Turner collection.* $275+.

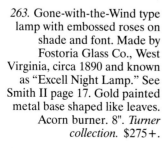

263. Gone-with-the-Wind type lamp with embossed roses on shade and font. Made by Fostoria Glass Co., West Virginia, circa 1890 and known as "Excell Night Lamp." See Smith II page 17. Gold painted metal base shaped like leaves. Acorn burner. 8". *Turner collection.* $275+.

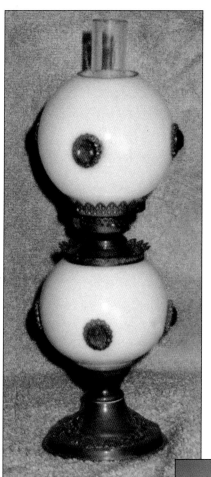

266. White milk glass lamp with ribbed brass pedestal foot. Pink flowers and green leaves on shade and base. Acorn burner. 7.5". *Lynch collection.* $300+.

264. White Bristol glass lamp with multi colored jewels in shade and base. Acorn burner. 9.5". *Weicksel collection.* $250+.

265. White milk glass embossed melon ribbed base and matching ball shade. Cigar lighter shade and burner. 8.25". *Gresko collection.* $200+.

268. China tree trunk with small branch handles and four log feet. Small branch stumps on the matching shade. Foreign burner. 6.75". *Author's collection.* $225+.

267. Gone-with-the-Wind type lamp. Fired-on purple painted flowers. Cast iron gold painted decorative base. "117210" marked on bottom. Similar to Smith I-304. "Twilight H B & H burner." 9". *Turner collection* $550+.

271. Porcelain base with four angels forming the feet. Acid etched ball shade depicts three Victorian ladies encased in a wreath design. P&A Victor burner. 9". *Author's collection.* $225+.

269. White Bristol glass. Orange decorated font, orange circled base. White shade with gold bands. Foreign burner. 9.75". *Author's collection.* $100+.

270. White Bristol lamp with decals of two kittens on shade and base. One has a blue ribbon, the other has bell and orange ribbon decoration. Foreign burner. 8". *Author's collection.* $125+.

272. White milk glass lamp with matching blue flowers with yellow centers, green leaves, and dark brown rays. Paint not fired on. Round string type burner. 6.75". *Etzel collection.* $300+.

273. Variant of Smith I-219 with a slightly smaller shade. Hornet burner. 9". *Turner collection.* $175+.

274. Small milk glass lamp with light green checkerboard design painted on the shade and base. 5.3". *Culver collection.* $250+.

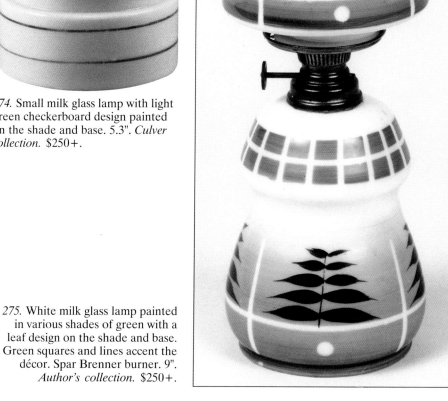

275. White milk glass lamp painted in various shades of green with a leaf design on the shade and base. Green squares and lines accent the décor. Spar Brenner burner. 9". *Author's collection.* $250+.

276. White milk glass
with maroon painted
geometric pattern.
Spar Brenner
burner. 7.75". *Zbar
collection.* $250+.

277. White milk glass lamp
with large green leaves
forming tree-shape on shade
and base. Spar Brenner
burner. 8.5". *Lynch collection.* $250+.

278. Milk glass base and
globe painted in circular
design of alternate
orange and blue flowers
separated by green
leaves on lime color
ground. Spar Brenner
burner. 8.5". *Plankinton
collection.* $300+.

280. White milk glass with embossed flowers painted maroon. Green leaves and scroll design. Bottom of shade and top of base also painted green. Acorn burner. 7.75". Also found in other color variations. *Cotting Collection*. $375+.

279. White milk glass decorated with raised enamel décor and bands of green and gold. Kosmos Brenner burner. 10.25". *Ruf collection*. $400+.

282. White milk glass lamp with embossed beads. Matching chimney shade decorated with red roses and pink ground. Hornet burner. 9". *Gresko collection.* $300+.

281. Milk glass embossed with drapery and scrolls. Similar to Hulsebus I-295 with this lamp being smaller and embossed on the shade. 8.4". *Culver collection.* $375+.

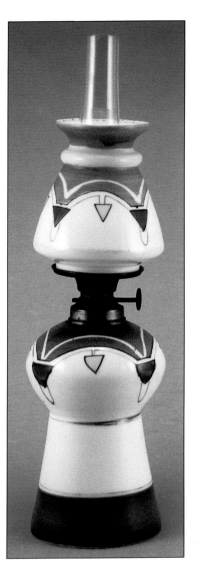

285. White milk glass with soft pink bands of color on shade and base. Gold lettering and leaf décor on shade "GOD NATT." Gold lettering missing on the base. Foreign burner. 6.5". *Author's collection.* $225+.

283. Milk glass lamp with hand painted teal background; geometric décor in maroon and yellow. Spar Brenner burner. 9.3". *Culver collection.* $325+.

284. Milk glass with blue fired-on paint highlight on the top and bottom of the base and shade. Painted "TOF GODT!" on the shade and "GOD NATT!" on the base. Spar Brenner burner. 8.1". *Culver collection.* $350+.

286. White milk glass lamp painted with blue dragonflies, green leaves, and maroon flowers. Spar Brenner burner. 9". *Author's collection.* $225+.

287. White Bristol glass. Hand painted blue and maroon flowers. Green leaves and gold band. Burner marked Lashbrenner. 8". *Author's collection.* $200+.

288. White Bristol lamp with pussy willow décor on shade and base in colors of gray, white, and black. White overshot paint on the base of shade; same overshot is painted tan on the base. Spar Brenner burner. 9.25". *Author's collection*. $250+.

289. White milk glass painted with fired-on light green background, purple and green flowers, green leaves. Spar Brenner burner. 7.75". *Zbar collection*. $250+.

290. White milk glass painted with deep green to light green to sky blue ground. Flowers and leaves painted in pink, yellow, and green. Spar Brenner burner. 8.5". *Zbar collection*. $300+.

293. White milk glass lamp with green bands circling the shade and base. Colorful red berries in alternate rows. Spar Brenner burner. 8". *Lynch collection.* $300+.

291. White milk glass lamp with green geometric design; thin green and gold bands circle the shade and base. Spar Brenner burner. 6". *Zbar collection.* $350+.

292. White Bristol glass decorated finger lamp with matching shade. The chimney is etched "R. Ditmar Wien," and the same name is on the string burner wheel. Foreign burner. 5.75". *Gresko collection.* $300+.

295. White milk glass lamp, green with white fired-on painted polka dots. Spar Brenner burner. 8.5". *Zbar collection.* $250+.

294. White milk glass with green and white polka dots. Spar Brenner burner. 8.5". *Lynch collection.* $300+.

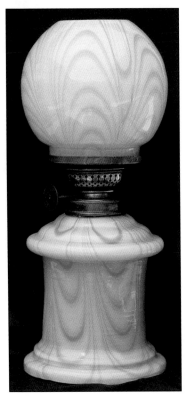

296. Opaque white glass cased in clear glass. Green looping design in shade and base. Cosmos Brenner burner. 10.5". *Zbar collection.* $400+.

298. White milk glass with fired-on cobalt blue painted ground. Red and light red painted flowers, green leaves. Spar Brenner burner, 8.5". *Zbar collection.* $350+.

297. Blue Bristol glass with painted flowers in white, green, maroon; green leaves and gold leaf pin striping detail. Spar Brenner burner. 8.75". *Zbar collection.* $350+.

300. White square milk glass base and ball shade decorated with birds and flowers. Gold gilded accents. Acorn burner. 8". *Ruf collection.* $350+.

299. Square pink marbleized milk glass font with round pink ball shade. Both decorated with violets. Acorn burner. 8.5". *Ruf collection.* $325+.

301. Custard colored milk glass with hand painted floral décor in dark rose and green leaves. Spar Brenner burner. 9.1". *Culver collection.* $350+.

302. White milk glass painted maroon with large white flowers and gilt leaf and wreath design. "Pat Feb'y 22 1877" on wick riser. 8.25". *Ruf collection.* $350+.

303. Cream satin glass with hand painted marigold and blue flowers trimmed with gold and white. Nutmeg burner. 8.75". *Baumgardner collection.* $325+.

304. White milk glass lamp with fired on paint in colors of rust and green. Spar Brenner burner. 9". *Zbar collection.* $350+.

305. White milk glass pedestal lamp with decorated base and matching ball shade. Hand painted pink flowers with green leaves. Spar Brenner burner. *Ruf collection.* $325+.

306. Porcelain lamp with embossed panels. Pink and green floral décor. Burner marked "EM & Co. The Boudoir." 9". *Lynch collection.* $500+.

309. White porcelain finger lamp with blue décor on shade and base. Spar Brenner burner. 8.5". *Zbar collection.* $450+.

307. White Bristol base and pink satin ball shade decorated with orange and blue flowers. Foreign burner. 6.5". *Gresko collection.* $400+.

308. Satinized white milk glass lamp with blue, yellow, and green floral décor. Half shade similar to Hulsebus I-142. Nutmeg burner. 7.5". Found with other color decoration. *McWright collection.* $450+.

310. White milk glass lamp. Fired-on flower decoration on ball type shade with pink ribbon round the top. High relief sprigs of fired-on blue and reddish flowers on pedestal type hexagonal base. Wick turner with geometrical decoration (Thiel & Bardenheuer, Ruhla). Foreign burner. 8.75". *Etzel collection.* $450+.

311. Cherub lamp with porcelain base and Bristol ball shade. Matching décor of cherubs and flowers in shades of pink, blue, flesh, and gold. Crystal light burner dated 1870, '71. 10.5". *Lynch collection.* $450+.

313. White milk glass with boats and landscape in brown tones. "Delft" on bottom. Eight pointed star on wick riser. 8.25". *Ruf collection.* $500+.

312. Porcelain embossed and scalloped base and shade. Both painted with purple flowers, green and brown leaves. Gold splattering to upper and lower parts of base. Kosmos Brenner burner. 11". *Wood collection.* $450+.

314. Delft decorated in colors of grayish blue in a matte finish with windmill and lake scenery. Lamp is unsigned. Base is decorated at the top with a leaf and flower design. Foreign burner. 10.5". *Hornwood collection.* $750+.

315. Blue Delft lamp. Porcelain base with white Bristol ball shade. Windmill and boat décor in shades of blue and gray. Prima Rundbrenner burner. 10.5". *Lynch collection.* $750+.

316. Delft-decorated white milk glass lamp. Shade pictures windmills beside water with boats. Base shows similar sights from a different perspective. Foreign burner. 11". *McWright collection.* $750+.

318. White Bristol glass Delft lamp with pear shaped base and ball shade. Green windmill and bird décor. Nutmeg burner. 9.5". *Lynch collection.* $500+.

317. Milk glass lamp with windmill scenes painted in mauve. Nutmeg burner. 8.5". *Plankinton collection.* $450+.

319. Blue and white Delft lamp. Windmill and water scenes in shades of blue. Four sided wedge shaped footed base. Bristol ball shade. Kosmos Brenner burner. 10.5". *Lynch collection.* $600+.

321. Decorated white milk glass lamp with brown and tan ground painted with a monk on base and ball shade. Nutmeg burner. 8". *Gresko collection.* $475+.

320. Small banquet lamp in blue Delft décor. Porcelain base marked "PG" in crossed swords with a crown and "St. Cloud" below the logo. Shade is white milk glass with windmill décor. E.M. Boudoir burner. 13". *Howard Smith collection.* $700+.

322. Stein lamp. Pottery mug style base with white milk glass floral embossed drop-in font and 4" ball shade. Green background with Monk transfer decoration on front side of shade and base; pipe on the back side. Number "12" painted on bottom of lamp. P&A Victor burner. 12.125". *Oldenlite II collection.* $1,350+.

323. Blue Bristol base and milk glass globe with painted design of a brown branch with orange flowers and buds and green leaves. Acorn burner. 9.5". *Plankinton collection.* $400+.

326. Milk glass lamp with pedestal shaped base. Fired on hand painted red and blue flowers. Spar Brenner burner. 9.4". *Culver collection.* $325+.

324. White Bristol lamp with décor of aqua, orange, purple garland. Brown bands painted on shade and base. Spar Brenner burner-shade holder. Refer to Smith II-369. 9". *Author's collection.* $350+.

325. White Bristol glass, with matching pink band and floral décor on shade and base. Gold leaf pin stripes. Spar Brenner burner. 8.5". *Zbar collection.* $350+.

329. White milk glass lamp with green leaves forming vines on shade and base. Saw-toothed edge at top of shade. Spar Brenner burner. 8". *Zbar collection.* $325+.

327. White milk glass with red, blue, green, brown, and orange flowers, leaves and vine. Blue and black dragonfly. Maroon paint on saw-toothed shade edge. Spar Brenner burner. 8.5". *Zbar collection.* $325+.

328. White milk glass lamp with blue flowers. Brown vines form a wreath that circles the shade and base. Saw-toothed edge on shade top may not be "original." Spar Brenner burner. 9". *Zbar collection.* $350+.

330. White milk glass lamp with various colors of blue leaves, brown vine, and rust colored berries. Blue paint outlines the saw-toothed shade edge. Spar Brenner burner. 7.5". *Author's collection.* $300+.

331. White milk glass painted with brown floral design. Scalloped shade. Pictured in *Lampor och Lampdelar,* Stockholm Sweden 1899, Fig. 345. Spar Brenner burner. 9". *Turner collection.* $400+.

151

332. White milk glass painted with mauve flowers, blue and green petals. Scalloped shade. Pictured in *Lampor och Lampdelar,* Stockholm Sweden 1899, Fig. 346. Foreign burner. 8". *Turner collection.* $400+.

333. White Bristol lamp with pink and maroon hand painted flowers and moss green leaves. Gold bands on shade and base with scalloped shade top. Spar Brenner burner. 9.25". *Author's collection.* $300+.

334. Grayish-tan colored lamp with rust colored enamel bands accented with white dots, rust colored vine, and green leaves. Shade top has saw-toothed edge. Spar Brenner burner. 8.5". *Author's collection.* $325+.

335. Pink Bristol glass lamp. Enameled floral décor in white, rust, and gray with gold highlights. Foreign burner. 10.75". *Oldenlite II collection.* $1,000+.

153

337. Satinized milk glass lamp with dark to light rose ground; colorful dogwood floral décor. Upturned shade slightly ruffled at the top. P&A Nutmeg burner. 7.5". *Culver collection.* $600+.

336. Pedestal style base, upturned ruffled shade in white Bristol glass painted in bright rust fading to white. Motif is of leaves in gold leaf, blue, purple, and brown. Spar Brenner burner. 12". *Zbar collection.* $800+.

340. White milk glass painted blue ground with heavy and slightly raised blue décor of mountains and trees in foreground. Ruffled shade. Spar Brenner burner. 8.5". *Zbar collection.* $400+.

338. White Bristol lamp with flowers in pink with a brown vine and bird, green leaves. Ruffled shade is outlined in gold. Similar to Smith II-359. Unmarked foreign burner requiring no chimney. 8.5". *Author's collection.* $425+.

339. White opaline finger lamp with matching ruffled chimney shade. Blue, orange, and green floral décor with gold highlights. Foreign burner. 9". *Oldenlite II collection.* $400+.

155

342. Bristol glass lamp with tan coloring on upper and lower shade and base. Mauve, yellow, green, and blue floral décor. Ruffled shade. Spar Brenner burner. 8.5". *Lynch collection.* $400+.

341. European clambroth Bristol glass stem lamp. Gold trim bands and enameled floral band on center of stem. White milk glass foreign shade with enameled floral band similar to that on lamp base. Mostly blue flowers on both. Spar Brenner burner with integral spider and 3" ring. 10.125". *McWright collection.* $400+.

343. Bristol-type white milk glass lamp with hand painted flowers in colors of pink and mauve. Green painted leaves. Upturned ruffled shade. Burner marked "Aufsteok Brenner." 9.75". *Cotting Collection.* $400+.

344. White Bristol milk glass with upturned highly ruffled shade. Sunflower motif with raised fired on enamel paint in red, blue, purple and yellow. Gold leaf accent. Foreign burner. 8". *Zbar collection.* $400+.

346. Milk glass painted blue shading lighter with gold lines, orange and blue flowers, and brown tone foliage. Upturned ruffled shade. Spar Brenner burner. 8.5". *Ruf collection.* $350+.

345. White Bristol glass with pink ground; mauve and blue pansy flowers connected by a brown branch circling both shade and base. Spar Brenner burner. 8". *Zbar collection.* $400+.

347. Tan custard glass lamp. Rust colored background with gold highlighted gray, brown, orange, and white floral décor. Spar Brenner burner. 10". *Oldenlite II collection*. $450+.

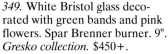

349. White Bristol glass decorated with green bands and pink flowers. Spar Brenner burner. 9". *Gresko collection*. $450+.

348. White milk glass painted pink and green with fired on design. Upturned ruffled shade. Pictured in *Lampor och Lampdelar,* Stockholm, Sweden 1899. Spar Brenner burner. 8.5". *Turner collection*. $425+.

352. Green opaque lamp has matching fired on gold leaf paint and fired-on enamel white and orange dot circle pattern. Gold leaf paint missing from the base. Spar Brenner burner. 8.5". *Zbar collection.* $400+.

350. White milk glass with pink and green paint depicting floral and geometric motif. Upturned ruffled shade. Spar Brenner burner. 8". *Zbar collection.* $400+.

351. Green opaque lamp has matching gold leaf paint, fired-on enamel white and orange dot circle pattern. Spar Brenner burner. 6.5". *Zbar collection.* $400+.

353. Green opaque milk glass lamp. Fired-on gold leaf and red paint decorative design and fired on enamel white dot circle pattern. Spar Brenner burner. 7.5". *Zbar collection.* $400+.

159

354. Green Bristol glass pedestal lamp with lightly ruffled shade which rests on the one piece shade ring holder. Small foreign burner. 9". *Author's collection.* $250+.

356. Blue Bristol glass lamp with tightly ruffled shade. Dark colored leaves; morning glory flowers on shade and base. Spar Brenner burner. Approximately 9". *Photo courtesy of Bill Young.* 600+.

355. Turquoise Bristol glass lamp with painted decorations in white, green, and burnt orange. Gold striping around top of shade and bottom of base. Burner marked Uno Flachbrenner. 8 5". *Cotting Collection.* $600+.

359. Set of transparent glass lamps. All have foreign burners and all are 7.5". Green lamp has swirled panels, red lamp has vertical panels in base, swirled in shade. Blue lamp has vertical swirled panels. Age questionable. *Zbar collection.* $75+ ea.

357. White milk glass with highly embossed ribs, beading, and leaves. Lavender, purple, and gold décor. Upturned ruffled shade. Spar Brenner burner. 8.5". *Author's collection.* $325+.

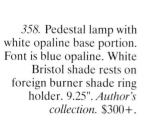

358. Pedestal lamp with white opaline base portion. Font is blue opaline. White Bristol shade rests on foreign burner shade ring holder. 9.25". *Author's collection.* $300+.

360. Arrangement of three transparent glass lamps in cobalt, emerald green, and ruby red. Heavy embossed grape leaf motif, these lamps were produced by the *Pukeberg Glassbruk* in Sweden. The three lamps have typical late 20th century foreign burners which are larger than the Spar Brenner, and take a wider diameter chimney than that used on the Spar Brenner. 9". Age questionable. *Zbar collection.* $125+ ea.

361. Arrangement of three lamps including an opaque aqua, white opaque, and orange opaque cased over white. Heavily embossed grape leaf motif. These lamps were produced by the *Pukeberg Glassbruk* in Sweden. The aqua lamp still has its label attached to the base. The three lamps have typical, late 20th century foreign burners which are larger than the Spar Brenner and take a wider diameter chimney than that used on the Spar Brenner. 9". Age questionable. *Zbar collection.* $125+ ea.

362. Green translucent glass lamp similar to Smith I-435. Swirl design in shade and base. 7.5". *Zbar collection.* $150+.

363. Green lamp with overshot decoration on the top of shade and lower portion of the base. White overshot flowers with green leaves and stems. Swirl design in shade; similar to Smith I-435. Foreign burner. 7.5". *Author's collection*. $125+.

365. Translucent amethyst lamp of foreign origin. Unmarked burner. 9.25". *Author's collection*. $225+.

364. Midnight blue lamp. Bulbous base and tall matching shade. Foreign unmarked burner. 9.25". *Author's collection*. $125+.

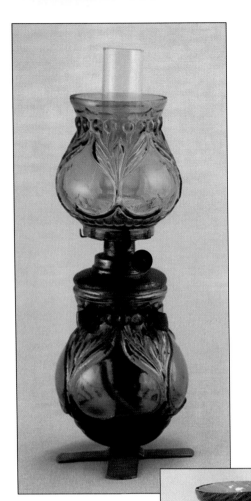

366. Green glass bracket lamp with embossed upside down heart shaped design. The metal bracket snaps over the base and is designed for resting upright as pictured, or hanging on a wall. Stern Brenner burner. 7.9". *Culver collection.* $400+.

368. Translucent green glass lamp with paneling design on the inside of both base and shade. 8.75". Unmarked burner. *Howard Smith collection.* $425+.

367. Cranberry embossed ribbed swirled base and matching shade. Foreign Burner. 7.15" *Fredrickson collection.* $400+.

369. Ruby cut lamp. Applied clear handle and egg shaped shade with matching scene of elk and trees. Reference Hulsebus I-230. Nutmeg burner. 8.5". *Lynch collection.* $300+.

370. Pair of transparent green and blue glass lamps with Spar Brenner burners. Both have frosted shades and glossy fonts. Swirl paneling in shades only. 9". *Zbar collection.* $325 green; $400. blue.

372. Transparent blue glass with vertical paneling. Spar Brenner burner. 9". *Zbar collection.* $500+.

373. Purple translucent glass with embossing. Square shaped base with ball-type shade. Spar Brenner burner. 9". *Turner collection.* $800+.

371. Emerald green lamp. Strong paneled design in shade and base. Spar Brenner burner. Approximately 10". *Photo courtesy of Bill Young.* $450+.

374. Green translucent glass base and ball
shade with strong paneling pattern.
Similar to Hulsebus I-208. Spar Brenner
burner. 8". *Turner collection.* $350+.

375. Cranberry glass footed lamp with
optic paneled base and shade. Nutmeg
burner. 10". *Fredrickson Collection.* $600+.

378. Cranberry swirled ribbed drum style base and ball shade with gold decoration. Foreign burner. 8". *McWright collection.* $1,325+.

376. Sapphire blue glass with an orange peel texture on both base and ball shade. Foreign burner. 6". *Goodger collection.* $500+.

377. Pigeon blood lamp on brass filigree pedestal base; pigeon blood shade and chimney. A brass font that fits into glass font secured by a central brass rod attached to base. Acorn burner. 8.25". *Goodger collection.* $425+.

168

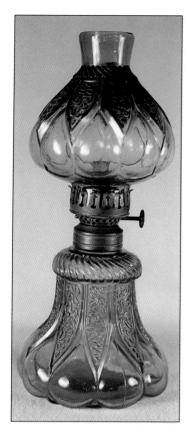

381. Blue opalescent base and chimney shade with optic paneling. Hornet burner. 8.5". *McWright collection.* $800+.

379. Blue glass lamp with embossed squiggles and reverse swirl ribbing. Shade has remains of unfired gold decoration. Hornet burner. 9.5". *Knox collection.* $550+.

380. Light amber shading to deep amber lamp. Slight panel design in the glass. Nutmeg burner. 8". *Author's collection.* $550+.

383. Deep ruby red glass, faint vertical panels slightly swirled in ruffled shade. Shade has been very slightly satinized from the midpoint down to soften and diffuse flame. Spar Brenner burner. 9" *Zbar collection.* $700+.

382. Translucent ruby red glass lamp with vertical swirled panels. Ruffled shade with slight iridescent, frosted sheen in middle portion to mute the flame. Spar Brenner burner. 9.5". *Zbar collection.* $700+.

384. Cobalt blue diamond impressed lamp. Upturned lightly ruffled shade. Spar Brenner burner. 9.5". *Ruf collection.* $700+.

385. "Daisey Lamp" in green Vaseline swirled glass with embossed metal base as shown in Spinning Wheel magazine 1958. "Daisey Lamp" burner. All original. 11.25" to top of shade. *Baumgardner collection.* $700+.

386. Cranberry peg lamp with panel design in both shade and base. Brass pegged font fits into ornate brass holder. Burner marked "Oxford Street Made in Germany." Collar numbered "5313" but burner is incorrect. 11.25". *Author's collection.* $700+.

387. White satin peg lamp. The shade sits in a glass tripod like Smith I-218 and the base is similar in shape to Smith I-326. Gold and tan decoration on shade, base, and column. The lamp fits into a white milk glass decorated candle-stick. Hornet burner. 14". *Gresko collection.* $850+.

171

388. Cranberry paneled glass peg lamp. Matching gold wreath décor on base and upturned ruffled shade. Kosmos Brenner burner. 11". *Lynch collection.* $850+.

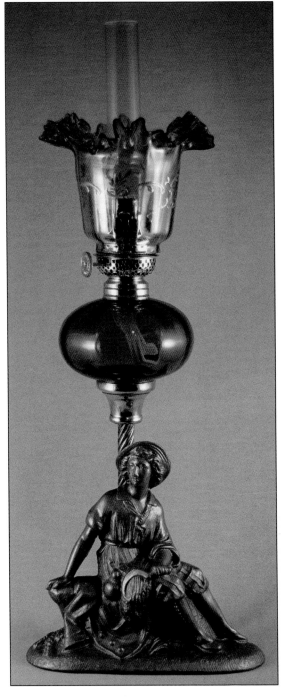

389. Cranberry pedestal lamp of a boy sitting on a rock. Spelter base, upturned ruffled shade with gold enamel decoration. P&A Victor burner. 15". *Lynch collection.* $800+.

392. Cranberry peg lamp slightly paneled with enameled decoration on the font and slightly ruffled upturned shade. Brass candlestick. Cosmos burner. 8" lamp only; 13" with candlestick. *Gresko collection.* $850+.

390. Textured glossy cranberry glass pegged font with acid-cut cranberry shade. Upturned ruffled shade with top edge finished in an appliqué of white satin glass. Foreign burner. 11". *McWright collection*. $1,200+.

391. Clear frosted pedestal lamp. Upturned ruffled shade with matching blue and gold embossed fleur-de-lis décor. Brass foot and stem. Kosmos Brenner burner. 13.5". *Lynch collection.* $650+.

395. Green satin and porcelain lamp. Highly embossed collar with leaves and berries. Gold wreath décor on upturned ruffled shade with matching brass décor on font. Triangular brass foot. Foreign burner. 12". *Lynch collection.* $700+.

393. Blue swirl mother-of-pearl peg lamp, font like Smith I-592 and with a matching shade that is round at the ruffled top. Cosmos burner. 11". *Gresko collection.* $2,000+.

394. Optic paneled shade and peg-style font in cranberry glass mounted on a brass candlestick. Foreign burner. 12.5". *McWright collection.* $900+.

396. Green satin glass paneled peg lamp. Heavy enameled leaves in rust, white, and gold. Upturned ruffled shade and apple shaped font. Kosmos burner. 10.5". *Lynch collection.* $750+.

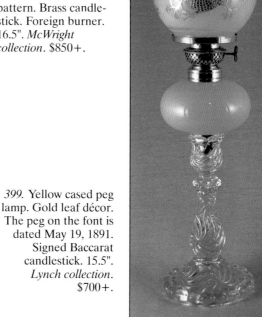

397. Pink cased glossy peg lamp. 5.5" half shade. Kosmos burner and spider. 14.5". *McWright collection*. $700+.

398. Rose shading to pink satin cased shade and matching peg font in a ribbed swirl pattern. Brass candlestick. Foreign burner. 16.5". *McWright collection*. $850+.

399. Yellow cased peg lamp. Gold leaf décor. The peg on the font is dated May 19, 1891. Signed Baccarat candlestick. 15.5". *Lynch collection*. $700+.

402. Sterling silver base with engraved leaves and decorative feet. Shade is frosted and embossed with a ribbed swirl design of blue and red flowers, green leaves, and white starburst enameled paint. Variant of Smith I-556. Unmarked foreign burner. 10.25". *Author's collection.* $1,000+.

401. Milk glass font and shade with painted silver lattice on a blue background. Matching child portraits on front and back of shade and font. Brass base, marble column. Kosmos style burner marked T R. 14". *Plankinton collection.* $1.600+.

400. Three-piece Jr. Banquet lamp. Rose Tiente base and font signed Baccarat Depose. Identically embossed red satin ball shade. Foreign burner. 18.725". *McWright collection.* $850+.

403. Silver base with ribbed swirled design. Blue opalescent upturned ruffled shade. Base is silver marked. Hinks burner. 10.5". *Author's collection.* $425+.

405. Silver plated base with raised medallion embossing on front and rear . Flat scalloped foot. P&A Victor burner and ring. Inverted blue spatter shade. Base hallmarked and alleged to be Gorham. 10.5". *McWright collection.* $650+.

404. Silver ribbed base signed "Mapin & Webb princes plate RE 71553" and stamped "W8604" and "Rd No 85697" numbers. Cranberry upturned shade with opalescent stripes, paneled pattern. Cranberry glass chimney. "Hinks & Son BIRM" burner. 9". *Turner collection* $750+.

406. Silver plated, heavily embossed base with floral and ribbon decorations. Amber ribbed, fluted shade with cream to white painted flowers. Kosmos Brenner burner. 10". *Baumgardner collection*. $600+.

408. Silver plated cone-shaped font on tripod feet with D-shaped handles. Hinks style burner and ring. Signed with a Z over a horn and "DB&S, EPBM 3667." Amberina hobnail shade probably by Stevens & Williams. 8.5". Mc*Wright collection*. $1,000+.

407. Silver plated cone shaped font on tripod feet with D-shaped handles. Hinks style burner and ring. Signed with a Z over a horn and "DB&S EPBM 3667." Reverse amberina shade. 8.5". *McWright collection*. $1,000+.

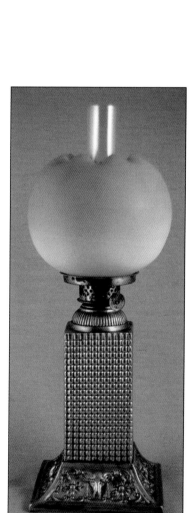

410. Bronze columns which support a font decorated with birds, phoenix and Foo dog on the base. Bristol decorated shade in colors of brown. Drop-in oil reservoir. Kosmos burner. 14.25". *Lynch collection.* $550+.

411. Brass Jr. Banquet lamp. Applied scroll-work on the body. Has drop-in font with P&A Victor burner. Embossed green overshot shade not original. 15.125". *McWright collection.* $450+.

409. Brass base with Burmese scalloped shade. P&A Victor burner. 9.5". *Howard Smith collection.* $800+.

412. Brass base with porcelain font. Font is painted dark blue with a cherub scene accented in gold. Acid etched shade is complimentary but not original. 12.75". *Howard Smith collection.* $550+.

414. Ivory colored base on metal stand. Metal arms attached to matching font decorated with three metal floral drapes and embossed metal top. Satin rose-lavender ball shade. Foreign burner. 12" to the top of the shade. *Ruf collection.* $600+.

413. Brass plated white metal Jr. Banquet lamp. Round bowl on four reeded legs. Drop-in font. Blue milk glass shade. P&A Victor burner. 13.75". *McWright collection.* $500+.

415. Banquet lamp with copper footed font, white milk glass shade, placed in a wrought iron stand with copper decorations. Kosmos Brenner burner. 16". *Ruf collection.* $700+.

416. Brass Jr. Banquet lamp wrought iron base painted black. Amber thumb print shade not original. P/A Victor burner 16" to top of shade. *Baumgardner collection.* $250+.

417. Cranberry French series lamp in a brass wire type stand. Cranberry chimney globe shade. Crystal finial on the bottom of the font. Foreign screw up burner. 15". *Gresko collection.* $600.00+.

420. Brass lantern-type lamp. Red glass with round coin spots made of applied glass. On the top, an owl is embossed in relief. The base and burner twist and lock into the glass. Burner marked "OEL BRENNER." 12.5". *Washka collection.* $400+.

418. Cranberry ribbed swirled shade and cone shaped font sitting in a black wrought iron holder. Foreign burner. 11". *Photo courtesy of Bill Young.* $800+.

419. Black iron base three font lamp with yellow fonts and shades. See Smith II-543. I believe this is the correct shade and base combination. Also found in blue, pink and white. P&A Victor burner. 12.5". *Cotting Collection.* $1,000+.

422. Porcelain banquet lamp. Impressed in the base is "6139." Floral decorated shade not original. P&A Victor burner. 14". *Ruf collection.* $350+.

421. Brass plated base of naked child holding brass font aloft. Brass openwork shade with cloth lining optional. Acorn burner. 12" to top of shade. *Privett collection.* $200+.

423. Porcelain Limoges Jr. Banquet; Elite France, yellow, pink, green, and gold floral decoration. P&A Victor burner. 13". *Baumgardner collection.* $450+.

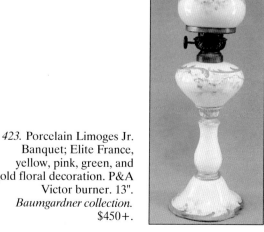

424. Banquet lamp in white milk glass with floral transfers on base and shade. P&A Victor burner. Chimney marked "PRIMA." 15.5". *Howard Smith collection.* $600+.

425. Three-tier Junior sized banquet lamp in pink milk glass. Shade, font, and base all have matching Fleur-de-lis décor. Same base as Smith II-421 except this lamp has oval-shaped shade. Metal base marked "58." P&A Victor burner. 17.6". *Howard Smith collection.* $900.

426. Yellow cased glass three-tier banquet lamp. P&A Victor burner. 18". *Howard Smith collection.* $750+.

427. Milk glass column Jr. Banquet lamp. Font and shade painted in blue-gray depicting a castle in a rural lakeside scene. Brass footed base marked "P&A79." P&A Victor burner. 17". *Plankinton collection.* $700+.

428. Milk glass column Jr. Banquet lamp. Font and shade of blue delft windmill in a rural lakeside scene. Brass footed base marked "P&A 79," P&A Victor burner. 17". *Plankinton collection.* $700+.

429. Jr. Banquet lamp with painted milk glass of green ground. Green, white, and gold floral décor. P&A Victor burner. 18". *McWright collection.* $500+.

430. Red satin glass banquet lamp with embossed design on shade and base as shown in Smith l-288. P&A Victor burner. 18.5". *Cotting collection.* $800+.

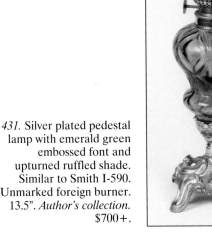

431. Silver plated pedestal lamp with emerald green embossed font and upturned ruffled shade. Similar to Smith I-590. Unmarked foreign burner. 13.5". *Author's collection.* $700+.

432. Azure blue glass lamp with embossed randomly repeating bursting swirls on base and shade. Brass pedestal base. Kosmos Brenner burner. 12.75". *Fredrickson Collection.* $750+.

435. Peg lamp in pale green iridized glass with paneled font. Matching shade forms eight petals of fired-on paint in colors of mauve flowers, green leaves with gold accents. Pewter footed base. Kosmos burner. 13". *Plankinton collection.* $800+.

433. Deep apricot shading to clear satin glass lamp. Acid cut back stylized flowers are matching on the font and shade. Kosmos Brenner burner. Cast metal foot. 12.5". *Fredrickson Collection.* $1,200+.

434. Pink iridized glass lamp with pot metal footed base. Gold bands circle shade and font. Enameled white flowers and green leaves. Approximately 11". Photo courtesy of *Bill Young.* $800+.

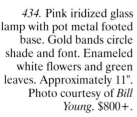

436. Cloisonne and Vaseline opalescent font with white Bristol shade. Cloisenné in colors of blue, white and wine. Foreign burner. 9". *Lynch collection.* $650+.

437. Smokey blue iridized lamp. White hand painted flowers and stems with pussy willow type décor. Gold accents; pink flower on both shade and base. Unmarked foreign burner. 6.5". *Author's collection.* $300+.

438. Green frosted glass lamp with enameled orange flowers and white flowery sprigs. Fired-on matte green leaves. Wick turner with stars forming a circle. 7.25". *Etzel collection.* $350+.

439. Clear glass with rust colored paint on top portion of shade and base. Small hand painted white and orange flowers and blue dots circling the lamp. Gold banding. Foreign unmarked burner. 8.25". *Author's collection.* $325+.

441. Clear glass with green paint on lower and upper portion of base and shade decorated with orange dots; white enamel dots form flowers. Gold bands on shade and base. Foreign burner. 7.5". *Author's collection.* $275+.

440. Pale blue satinized glass lamp with gold banding. Décor of white dots that represent flowers with orange centers and gold loops. Stern Brenner burner. 6.5". *Etzel Collection.* $325+.

444. Frosted glass lamp with orange ground. Enameled floral décor on shade and base. Foreign burner. 7". Photo courtesy of *Bill Young*. $350+.

442. Clear glass overshot thistle flowers in red, with green leaves, black stems. All flowers trimmed in gold. Foreign burner. 8". *Wood collection.* $350+.

443. Pale olive green iridized glass lamp with small panels of overshot on base and shade. White enamel dots form flowers and gold with black vertical and horizontal bands add to décor. Spar Brenner burner. 8.5". *Author's collection* $325+.

445. Soft pink satin glass with hand painted bell-shaped flower on base and shade. Foreign burner. 7.3". *Judy White collection*. $300+.

446. Green translucent lamp with hand painted large red tulips, green stems. Spar Brenner burner. 8". *Zbar collection.* $400+.

447. Emerald green glass lamp with gold décor. Tiny blue dots formed to resemble flowers. Foreign burner. 5.25". *Author's collection.* $625+.

448. Cranberry lamp with very ornate gold paint décor. Minute blue and white dots to resemble flowers. Gold scroll design. Possibly Moser. Foreign burner. 5.5". *Author's collection.* $700.

450. Vasa Murrhina glass. Clear with white, pink, red, and silver spatters. Unmarked foreign burner. Similar to Smith II-512. 6.5". *Author's collection.* $525+.

449. Green glass with very ornate gold gilding design on shade and base. Small foreign burner. 6.5". *Author's collection.* $625+.

451. Pale green glass lamp trimmed in gold décor with pale pink flowers painted on the gold background. Nutmeg burner. 7". *Plankinton collection.* $500+.

453. Light blue translucent glass lamp with raised, fired-on flower and vine motif in white, blue, yellow, and brown enamel paint. Spar Brenner burner. 7.5". *Zbar collection.* $550+.

452. Emerald green lamp with white dots that form flowers in a garland around the shade and base. Faint traces of a gold band on both pieces. Spar Brenner burner. 6". *Author's collection.* $500+.

454. Translucent blue glass with white fired-on enameled paint depicting flowers and leaves circling shade and base. Vertical orange enamel dots and gold leaf pin striping separating painted areas. Spar Brenner burner. 8". *Zbar collection.* $400+.

456. Translucent blue glass lamp with white fired-on enamel paint depicting flowers and leaves, with dots down the sides between painted scenes. Gold leaf pin stripes. Foreign burner. 7.5". *Zbar collection.* $450+.

455. Blue glass with white enameled décor. Base and shade are ribbed on the inside. Spar Brenner burner. 9". *Culver collection.* $450+.

457. Translucent glass lamps. Both have white
fired on enamel paint with orange dots and gold
leaf pin stripes and accents. Blue lamp has slight
vertical panels swirled in shade. Both have glossy
finish on base; frosted shades. Both have Spar
Brenner burners. Blue 9"; green 8.75". *Zbar
collection.* $450+ ea.

458. Translucent
smokey blue lamp with
white enamel painted
flowers and leaves.
Spar Brenner burner.
9.25". *Author's
collection.* $450+.

459. Translucent cranberry base
with frosted ball shade. Both base
and shade painted with white floral
design. See Fig. 347 in *Lampor och
Lampdelar,* Stockholm, Sweden
1899. Spar Brenner burner. 9".
Turner collection. $450+.

462. Green glass with white enameled flowers and leaves; shade and base are paneled. Foreign burner embossed "H/B." 7". *Wood collection.* $400+.

460. Emerald green lamp with bands of gold on shade and base. Gold hand painted flowers and scroll highlighting shade and base. Spar Brenner burner. 10". *Author's collection.* $350+.

461. Light green glass decorated with gold enameling and a matching chimney shade. Unmarked burner. 6.5". *Gresko collection.* $450+.

463. Blue glass lamp. White hand painted garland of leaves and flowers with red dot centers. Spar Brenner burner. 9.25". *Author's collection.* $400+.

464. Iridized frosted marigold lamp. Tight ruffled shade. Colorful purple flowers and green leaves. Foreign burner. 8.5". *Lynch collection.* $400+.

465. Rose to green satin glass lamp. Enameled decoration of white, blue, and gold flowers, green and white foliage. Gold trimmed ruffled upturned shade. 8.75". *Etzel collection.* $500+.

467. Green iridized lamp with heavy gold decoration of a wreath and flower. Upturned ruffled shade. Similar to Hulsebus I-203. Foreign burner. 7.5". *Author's collection.* $475+.

466. Clear glass lamp with frosted bluish-green ground. Enameled yellow and green floral décor. Gold highlights on the shade ruffled edge. Foreign burner. 6.125". *Oldenlite II.* $600+.

468. Cobalt "Mary Gregory" type lamp with up-turned ruffled shade. White fired-on cherubs. Slight swirl glass pattern. Spar Brenner burner. 9.5". *Turner collection.* $800+.

198

470. Midnight blue glass lamp with gold leaves and white dots to resemble flowers with orange centers. Ruffled chimney globe shade. Hornet burner. 10.5". *Author's collection.* $600+.

469. Cranberry glass lamp with applied white enamel flowers and foliage. Up-turned tightly ruffled shade. Spar Brenner burner. 9". *Ruf collection.* $800+.

471. Clear paneled lamp with rose coloring on upper and lower portion of shade and base. Small white enamel dots form flowers with orange centers. Gold striping décor. Spar Brenner burner. Approximately 8.5". *Photo courtesy of Bill Young.* $600+.

472. Rose iridescent lamp with white enamel décor of tiny dots resembling a bow. Similar to Hulsebus I-202. Spar Brenner burner. Approximately 8". *Photo courtesy of Bill Young.* $600+.

473. Vaseline opalescent glass lamp. Enameled white flowers and long green leaves painted with gold trim. Ruffled up-turned shade similar to Smith I-521. Spar Brenner burner. 9". *Turner collection.* $1,500+.

474. Blue translucent glass lamp with white fired-on decoration. A band of rick-rack design on shade and base with white floral décor. Stern Brenner burner. 7.5". *Etzel Collection.* $500+.

475. Translucent emerald green lamp with vertical panels and ruffled shade. White and yellow raised fired-on enamel leaf and geometric design with gold leaf leaves and detail. Spar Brenner burner, 9.5". *Zbar collection.* $450+.

476. Amber glass lamp paneled inside. Decorated with enameled daisies on the base and matching upturned ruffled shade. Spar Brenner burner. 9". *Gresko collection.* $600+.

477. Blue translucent glass with white, gray, and orange raised fired-on enamel paint depicting leaves, flowers, and designs. Vertical panels and up-turned ruffled shade. Gold leaf pin striping. Spar Brenner burner. 9". *Zbar collection.* $600+.

479. Translucent blue glass lamp with slight vertical paneling. Ruffled shade and pedestal type base. Spar Brenner burner. 10". *Zbar collection.* $600+.

478. Cranberry glass with hand painted enameled geometric design on both the upturned ruffled shade and pedestal type base. Similar to Hulsebus I-219. Faint paneling design in the glass. Spar Brenner burner. 9.75". *Goodger collection.* $650+.

480. Blue decorated lamp. Small white painted dots to represent flower and leaves. Tight crimped ruffled shade on Spar Brenner burner. 9.5". *Author's collection.* $600+.

482. Clear glass with blue iridized color on shade and base. White dots form flowers; green leaves, blue bird with orange beak on base and ruffled matching shade. Unmarked foreign burner. 8.5". *Author's collection.* $600+.

481. Textured glass lamp with amethyst coloring on top of base and ruffled shade. Enamel painted farmhouse scene and foliage with blue mountains. Décor is similar to Hulsebus I-333/ 334. Unmarked foreign burner. 7.75". *Author's collection*. $700+.

483. Blue milk glass with ball shade. Foreign burner. 9" high. *McWright collection*. $350+.

484. Cased pink milk glass with cylindrical base. Shade has soft scallops at the top. Foreign burner. 9.5". *Howard Smith collection.* $425+.

485. Blue cased lamp with inverted, tightly ruffled shade. Base and shade lined white. Vertical pattern of fletches on base and shade. Hornet burner. 10.5". *McWright collection.* $1,600+.

486. Pink cased glass lamp. Tapered square base embossed with scrollwork plus a flower in each panel. Elliptical, six paneled shade with scalloped top edge. Each panel contains an embossed floral spray. Foreign burner. 8.5". *McWright collection.* $1,800+.

487. Yellow glossy cone lamp variant of Smith 1-394 with filigree that goes over the collar and is fitted to the contours of the base. Nutmeg burner. 7.75". *Gresko collection.* $800+.

205

488. Pink satin pansy ball cased light pink inside with filigree on the entire base. A variant of Smith I-389. Nutmeg burner. 6.5". *Gresko collection.* $950+.

490. Rose satin glass melon ribbed finger lamp with matching shade. The shade has a scalloped rim. White milk glass applied handle. Foreign Burner. 9.5". *Hornwood collection.* $1,000+.

489. Blue milk glass with silver filigree. A variant of Smith II-249. Hornet burner. 9". *Baumgardner collection.* $650+.

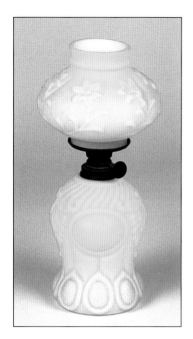

491. White to yellow satin lamp with two large embossed horizontal ovals on the font, six smaller vertical ovals around the base and two large stylized leaves. The shade is embossed with single flowers on single stems. Spar Brenner burner. 8.75". *Ruf collection.* $850+.

493. Rose shading to light pink satin vertically ribbed lamp. Cylindrical shaped base with slightly elongated ball shade. In addition to being ribbed, the shade has two horizontal raised bands. The base is dome shaped with two raised windows and two raised doors embossed on its sides. Foreign burner. 8.5". *McWright collection.* $2,100+.

492. Blue opaline base with matching satinized shade. Burner marked Spar Brenner. 6.75". *Author's collection.* $400+.

494. Trio of transparent glass lamps with embossed geometric design. Manufactured by Pukeberg Glassbruk in Sweden around 1905. From left deep blue, light green, and emerald green. All have glossy bases and frosted shades, and this is likely the original form. See Hulsebus I-193. Spar Brenner burners. 9". *Zbar collection.* $800 blue and emerald green. $700 light green.

495. Chartreuse to white cased glass satinized with white lining. Shade is embossed with decorative geometric design. Spar Brenner burner. 8.5". *Zbar collection.* $1,800+.

496. Cranberry finger lamp with slight paneling in shade and base. Top of shade has soft scalloped edge. 8.25". *Hornwood collection.* $750+.

497. Yellow opalescent melon shaped lamp. Applied crystal handle. Foreign burner. 7.5". *King Collection.* $600+.

499. Cranberry paneled lamp. Shade similar in shape to Smith II-506. Spar Brenner burner. 8.25". A*uthor's collection.* $800+.

498. Amethyst finger lamp with applied handle. Oval shaped satin finished chimney shade with lavender highlighting. Matching sprays of violets as is on the base. Raised enamel beadwork with gold tracery. Base has raised enamelwork violets. Foreign burner. 6". *Fredrickson collection.* $350+.

500. Cranberry opalescent striped lamp similar to Smith II-506. Spar Brenner burner. 8.75". *Author's collection.* $900+.

501. Light green opalescent lamp with optic design in shade and base. Upturned ruffled shade. Foreign burner. 8.75". *Hornwood collection.* $800+.

503. Cranberry to clear paneled lamp. Pedestal type base, umbrella shade. Nutmeg burner. 9". *Ruf collection.* $800+.

502. Baccarat reverse swirl Rose Tiente base. Indented four sided ruffled topped shade with acid etched embossing. Top 1/3 lightly colored to match base. Paper label on shade reads "Baccarat France." Foreign burner. 10.75". *Knox collection.* $500+.

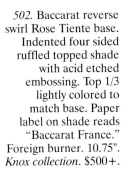

504. Pair of identical lamps in transparent green and cranberry glass with frosted shades, glossy fonts. Embossed leaf and flower pattern. See Smith I-407. Spar Brenner burner. 8". *Zbar collection.* $650+ ea.

505. Yellow and white marbled pattern lamp with glossy finish. Spar Brenner burner. 8". *Zbar collection.* $1000+.

506. Vaseline glass with up-turned opalescent ruffled shade. Applied decoration around base. Round string type burner. Wick turner with shaded star design marked "Ehrich & Graetz, Berlin." 6.5". *Etzel collection.* $900+.

507. Cranberry glass base with three clear applied handles. Color of the eight pointed shade varies from cranberry to almost clear. Spar Brenner burner. 7". *Plankinton collection.* $1,600+.

509. Rubina glass lamp with swirl design in shade and base. Shade is satin glass whereas the base is not. Spar Brenner burner. 8.5". *Author's collection.* $900+.

508. White opalescent lamp with slight paneling design in the glass. Clear applied rigaree curly-cue on the sides of both shade and base. Spar Brenner burner. 7.5". *Author's collection.* $900+.

510. Pink translucent crackle glass with upturned opalescent ruffled shade. Spar Brenner burner. 8.5". *Zbar collection.* $950+.

512. Opalescent Vaseline translucent glass with vertical stripes in base and shade . Upturned ruffled shade. Spar Brenner burner. 9". *Zbar collection.* $1800+.

511. Opalescent Vaseline translucent glass with vertical swirled stripes in base and shade. Upturned ruffled shade. Spar Brenner burner. 9". *Zbar collection.* $1,900+.

514. Vaseline glass lamp with white "looping" design in base and shade. Slightly different than preceding lamp in width and design. Spar Brenner burner. 9.5". *Author's collection.* $1,800+.

513. White Bristol glass lamp with red "looping" design in base and shade. Upturned ruffled shade. Spar Brenner burner. 9.25". *Author's collection.* $2,000+.

515. Dark cranberry with an orange peel texture on the outside of the glass on both the base and matching shade. Prima burner. 11". *Howard Smith collection.* $500+.

516. Blue to clear satin glass lamp with square base and ball shade. Slight panel design in both shade and base. Foreign burner. 10.25". *Author's collection.* $700+.

518. Opaque cased glass with swirl peppermint stripe pattern. Coloration is consistent pink and white pattern in base, light to darker pink in shade. Satin finish base and shade. Shade is upturned and highly ruffled. Reverse swirl between base and shade. Spar Brenner burner. 10". *Zbar collection.* $1,600+. *(519 shows a very similar lamp.)*

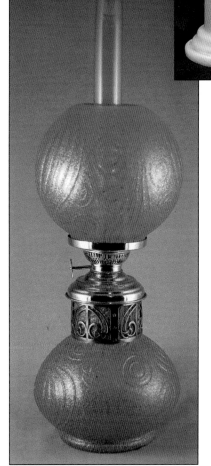

517. Cranberry overshot lamp with embossed pattern on base and ball shade. Nickel drop-in font. Silver filigree around top of glass base. Nickel Kosmos Brenner burner. 12". *Lynch collection.* $1,500+.

519. Opaque glass, with swirl peppermint stripe pattern. Coloration is consistent pink and white pattern in base and shade. Satin finish base and shade. Shade is upturned and highly ruffled. Spar Brenner burner. 9.5". *Zbar collection*. $1,600+.

521. Raspberry shading to pale pink satin glass lamp with embossed stylized tulip décor. Spar Brenner burner. 8.5". *Oldenlite II collection*. $1,800+.

520. Pink shading to raspberry satin glass embossed lamp. Ruffled shade. Embossed leaf design forms a four sided shade and base. Spar Brenner burner. 8.75". *Author's collection*. $1,800+.

522. Dark pink shading to paler color satin glass lamp. Highly embossed pattern of leaves and scrolls. Upturned ruffled shade. P&A Victor burner. Approximately 11". *Photo courtesy of Bill Young.* $1,600+.

523. Pink satin shading to white embossed lamp. White cased lining. Shade slightly ruffled. Kosmos Brenner burner. 12.5". *Ruf collection.* $900+.524

524. Yellow glass with soft crackle glass effect . Leaf embossing on shade and base accented in gold. Spar Brenner burner. 9". *Washka collection.* $1,200+.

525. Amethyst lamp
with upturned ruffled
crimped shade. Spar
Brenner burner. 9.5".
Fredrickson collection.
$800+.

526. Blue satin cased glass
diamond-quilted-mother-of-
pearl lamp with upturned
ruffled shade. Similar to Smith
I-Fig. IX. Foreign Burner. 8".
King collection. $2,500+.

527. Deep blue
diamond pattern satin
glass lamp with ruffled
shade. 7.75" Similar to
Smith I Fig. IX. Spar
Brenner burner. 7.75".
Turner collection.
$2,500+.

528. Monet Stumpf Pantin lamp with square base. Soft panel design in shade and base. Dark pink shading to opalescent. Foreign burner. 9.5". *Author's collection.* $1,800+.

529. Pink and white opalescent glass with shades of gold. Matching glass fluted up-turned shade. Similar to Smith II-509. Kosmos burner. 10". *Turner collection.* $1,600+.

532. Blue opalescent lamp with applied feet. Matching opalescent tightly crimped ruffled shade. Matching blue opalescent chimney. Spar Brenner burner. 6.5". *Author's collection.* $2,000+.

530. Pink and white opalescent glass with up-turned shade. Base has swirled and ribbed pattern, shade has subtle paneling and swirl pattern. Kosmos burner. 10". *Turner collection.* $1,600+.

531. Yellow glossy glass with ball font and crystal applied feet. Shade is flared four ways similar to Smith1-524, and has a pale yellow top shading down to bright yellow. Nutmeg burner. 7.75". *Gresko collection.* $1,700+.

533. Amberina with slight panel design in shade and base. Amber feet and leaves on base. Nutmeg burner. Shown in Smith II-495. 8". *Oldenlite II collection.* $2,800+.

534. Amber hobnail lamp with umbrella shade and amber applied feet. Similar to Hulsebus I-395. Nutmeg burner. Amber chimney optional. 8.5". *Morell collection.* $1,400+.

535. Cranberry diamond shape ribbed swirled font with four clear knob feet. Cranberry shade and cranberry paneled chimney. Dietz Davis & Co., London burner. 9" to top of shade. 12" to top of chimney. *Ruf collection.* $1,650+.

536. Blue diamond quilted mother-of-pearl with a rounded base and ruffled shade rounded at the top. Foreign burner. 6.25". *Gresko collection.* $2,300+.

537. Pink and blue vertical striped satin glass lamp. Upturned ruffled shade. Small foreign burner. 5.5". *Author's collection.* $3,000+.

539. Pink diamond pattern cased glass lamp with applied clear glass prunts. Cranberry chimney may not be original. Spar Brenner burner. 7". *Bridges collection.* $2,875+.

538. Green satin glass lamp in diamond-quilt-mother-of-pearl pattern. Small foreign burner. 5.5". *Author's collection.* $2,300+.

540. Spatter glass lamp in colors of orange, pink, white, and yellow. Base has clear glass applied feet. Upturned tightly ruffled shade. Nutmeg burner. 8". *Author's collection.* $2,200+.

541. Yellow ribbed swirl base with clear applied ruffle around bottom with matching smooth upturned ruffled shade. Butler marked burner. 6.5". *Ruf collection.* $2,000+.

542. Raspberry to pink satin glass Mother-of-Pearl lamp with soft ruffled upturned shade. P&A Victor burner. Approximately 10.5". *Photo courtesy of Bill Young.* $1,800+.

543. Yellow satin glass Mother-Of-Pearl in raindrop pattern. Frosted applied shell feet. Nutmeg burner. Similar to Smith II-524. 8.25". *Author's collection.* $1,600+.

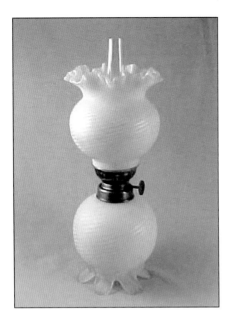

544. Yellow shading to white satin glass Mother-of-Pearl swirl lamp with applied feet and ruffled shade. Foreign burner. 10.5". *Cotting collection.* $1,800+.

546. Vaseline opalescent swirl lamp. Shade crimps in at the shoulder. Base has four wide splayed feet in pink Unmarked foreign burner. 8.25". *Author's collection.* $1,800+.

545. Pink opalescent ribbed with enameled flowers on the base and matching shade. Crystal rigaree around the base forming a skirt. Cosmos burner. 11". *Gresko collection.* $2,400+.

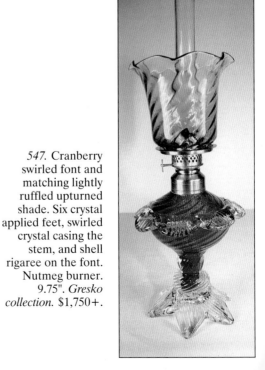

547. Cranberry swirled font and matching lightly ruffled upturned shade. Six crystal applied feet, swirled crystal casing the stem, and shell rigaree on the font. Nutmeg burner. 9.75". *Gresko collection.* $1,750+.

548. Rubina overshot glass. Upturned ruffled shade. Base has ribbed pattern with applied shell feet forming a skirt. Foreign burner. 9". *Turner collection.* $2,500+.

550. Peach shading to orange opalescent lamp with large honeycomb pattern in the shade and base. Upturned ruffled shade. Clear glass applied petals form a skirt at the base. Kosmos Brenner burner. 9.25". *Author's collection.* $2,000+.

549. Lime green shading to clear overshot glass lamp. The three clear applied looped feet form a design continuing up the font. Spar Brenner burner. 9.75". Also found in Cranberry. *Ruf collection.* $2,000+.

551. Cranberry glass lamp with optic paneling in shade and base. Clear glass applied feet forming a skirt around base. White enamel floral décor. Spar Brenner burner. 8". *Bridges collection.* $1,800+.

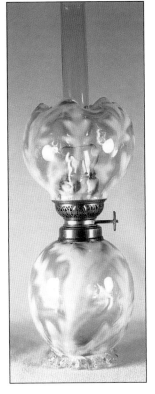

553. Satin glass lamp in raspberry shading to light pink diamond-quilt-mother-of-pearl pattern. Applied frosted crystal feet. Foreign burner. 9.5". *Oldenlite II collection.* $1,800+.

`552. Light blue opalescent glass lamp with opalescent leaf patterning. Rose bowl style shade. Applied crystal rigaree foot. See Smith I-567 for overshot version. Foreign burner. 10". *Oldenlite II collection.* $2,800+.

554. Cranberry glass with faint vertical paneling. Upturned square ruffled shade. Applied clear glass 'wings' and feet. Spar Brenner burner. 9". *Zbar collection.* $1,250+.

556. Cranberry to clear overshot lamp with five applied crystal feet. Foreign burner. 9.5". *Oldenlite II collection.* $1,600+.

555. Pink opalescent ribbed lamp. Green applied feet. Upturned ruffled shade. Hinks burner. 9". *Lynch collection.* $2,700+.

557. Cranberry lamp with slight paneling in the glass. Tall clear glass applied feet. Tightly ruffled upturned shade. Kosmos burner. 9.5". *Author's collection.* $1,800+.

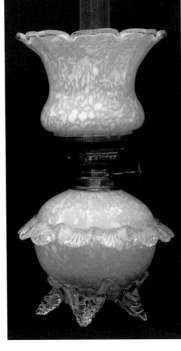

558. Cranberry glass lamp with optic paneling in shade and base. Clear glass applied feet. Foreign burner. 9.5". *Bridges collection.* $2,500+.

560. Cased yellow glass lamp with white spatter. It has an applied crystal edge at the top of the shade and 6 applied crystal feet. Spar Brenner burner. 9.50". *Oldenlite II collection.* $2,500+.

559. Pink to light pink cased glass with marbled patterned glossy finish. Applied clear glass shell rigaree around shoulder of the font. Applied clear glass feet. Cosmos burner. 9.5". *Zbar collection.* $2,500+.

561. Nailsea style cranberry glass lamp with white loopings. Applied crystal rigaree and pedestal base with tooled petal foot. Foreign burner. 10". *Oldenlite II collection*. $3,500+.

562. Satinized pale green glass shading to white. Green ruffled edge on shade; applied frosted rigaree on shoulder of base. Foreign burner. 10". *Oldenlite II collection*. $1,500+.

563. Cranberry glass lamp with Vaseline applied feet and flared edges to top of the shade. Foreign made. Spar Brenner burner. 8.75". *Keathley collection.* $2,000+.

565. Marigold colored satin glass shade and font resting on a green lily-pad leaf foot. Strong vertical paneled design. Probably Stevens and Williams. Scalloped shade top. Approximately 8.5". Foreign burner. *Photo courtesy of Bill Young.* Price unavailable.

564. Cranberry translucent glass shading to white opalescent glass in shade. Faint vertical panels throughout. Highly worked upturned shade with out-turned flipped tips. Spar Brenner burner. 9". *Zbar collection.* $1,800+.

566. Cranberry clear glass with embossed decorations and applied Vaseline feet. Smith I-425 variant. Acorn burner. 10". *Turner collection.* $1,000+.

567. Cranberry lamp with embossed ribbed swirl pattern. Eight applied zipper pattern Vaseline feet with ruffled, crimped matching applied border on top of shade. Spar Brenner burner. 8.75". *Fredrickson Collection.* $2,200+.

570. Pink opalescent font surrounded by four bud vases mounted on an eight-pointed apple green foot. Front side of base adorned with a 2.75" pink opalescent flower and multiple green leafs. This is much the same décor as seen on Smith-522. Pink opalescent optic paneled inverted shade. Foreign burner. 10". *McWright collection.* $2,500+.

568. Rainbow mica flecked peg lamp with overshot shade. Opaque panels of blue, yellow, and red in both the shade and font. Up-turned tightly ruffled shade. Probably French. Burner riser marked with symbols and word "Paris." 7". *Ruf collection.* $3,000+.

569. Yellow glass with white marble swirl pattern. Jack-in-the-pulpit type shade. Amber colored applied feet. Shade similar to Smith I-461. Sternbrenner burner. 6.5". *Turner collection.* $2,300+.

571. Finely ribbed pale pink opalescent petal top shade and base. Applied crystal leaf style feet and rigaree on shoulder of the base. Foreign burner. 12.125". *Oldenlite II collection.* $2,500+.

572. Light green glass with white opalescent dotted stripes. Applied green glass leaf style feet. Foreign burner. 9.5". This lamp originally had matching opalescent Hinks style chimney. *Oldenlite II collection.* $2,500+.

574. Cut glass leaded crystal lamp with petal style foot. Foreign burner marked "Messenger's BIRM." 11.5". *Oldenlite II collection.* $5,000+.

573. Amber threaded glass lamp with upturned ruffled shade. Clear glass applied feet. Spar Brenner burner. Approximately 9". *Photo courtesy of Bill Young.* $2,000+.

575. Deep raspberry satin glass diamond quilted-mother-of-pearl with yellowish air traps; three applied opaque feet and matching conical shade. Possibly Webb. Burner marked "The Silber Light Comp." 8.25". *Ruf collection.* $2,200+.

576. Bronze shading to cream satin glass lamp in diamond quilted mother-of-pearl pattern. Conical shaped shade. Lamp attributed to Webb. Spar Brenner burner. 9". *Author's collection.* $3,000+.

577. Yellow shading to pink cased glass lamp with heavy gold enamel paint floral décor. Pale blue cased lining, slightly ruffled shade. Thought to be Webb. Foreign burner. 10.5". *Bridges collection.* $5,500+.

578. Yellowish diamond quilted mother-of-pearl satin glass lamp. The base is gold gilded with four cherubs hiding the support post for the font. Embossed platform with four feet and posts. Upturned ruffled shade. Kosmos Brenner burner. 11". *Author's collection.* $3,000+.

579. Vaseline Nailsea three piece lamp with upturned ruffled shade. Curled clear applied glass feet. Matching Nailsea chimney scalloped at the top. Duplex burner. Attributed to White Friars Glass Works, London by James Powell in the 1880s. 11.25" to top of shade. *Authors collection.* $6,000+.

580. Webb cameo glass lamp in duBarry pink and white. Foreign burner. 9.5". *McWright collection.* $12,500+.

581. Citron Cameo glass lamp with matching carved flowers and leaves in the base and shade. Carved butterfly design on the base. Conical shaped shade. Lamp unsigned but purported to be Thomas Webb. Similar to Hulsebus I-432. Burner marked "The Silber Lamp Co." 8.5". *Author's collection.* $10,000+.

Contemporary Lamps

582. Gone-with-the-Wind style lamp in Latticino glass; colors of pink, red, green, blue, and yellow stripes. This is sometimes referred to as Ribbon Glass. Nutmeg burner. 11.125". $425. Smaller version of Latticino glass lamp in identical colors. 4". *Lawrence collection.* $350.

584. Millefiori glass lamps with umbrella style shades. Left, dark background with light colored canes. Center, multi colored canes. Right, blue with white colored canes. Nutmeg burner. 7.75". *Lawrence collection.* $375.

583. Gone-with-the-Wind style lamp in Millefiori glass. Left, gold colored background and white canes. Center, dark background with multi-colored canes. Right, blue background with white canes. Nutmeg burner. 10.5". *Lawrence collection.* $600, $375, $375 respectively.

585. Three sizes of Millefiori. Left, yellow is 10.5".
Center, multi-color is 7.75". Right, blue is 4.75".
Lawrence collection. Priced above.

586. Finger lamps in various glass and colors. Left, multi-colored
Millefiori. Center, red Latticino. Right, blue Millefiori. Gem Hornet-
style burner. 9" to top of the chimney. *Lawrence collection.* $175.

238

Fluid Burning Related Items

a. Brass lamp used to light instruments, i.e. a ship's compass. From Australia, possibly English. 3.25" tall x 1.5" round. *Turner collection.* $75+.

d. Pewter cigar lighter lamp with brass trimming on the brimmed hat, epaulets, and highlights on the shirt, jacket, and base. Probably English. Boy's brass cigar has a wick. The placard at the base reads "Le Premier Essai." 6". *Hornwood collection.* $400+.

b. Cylindrical emerald and ruby jeweled hanging lamp with removable font. Silver plated. 8". *Baumgardner collection.* $175+.

e. Silver flying swan with great detail. Round wick type burner with snuff-cap. 5" tall with 5.5" wing span. *Turner collection.* $100+.

c. Owl cigar lamp. Clear glass base with panels. Silver head and jeweled yellow eyes. Round wick burner on top of head. Ears pull out to light cigars. 4". *Turner collection.* $200+.

f. Silver plated pocket watch marked Folmer & Schwing "Watch Pocket Lamp" with embossed design on outside. Patent dates June 23, July 21, 1891; 3.125" to top of ring. *Privett collection.* $100+.

g. Little brass finger lamp embossed on bottom "E.F. Rogers Patent Jan. 30, 1866." String wick. 3.5". *Cotting Collection.* $75+.

j. Black glass font with pewter top. 2.75" to top of collar and 3.5" to top of tube. *Ruf collection.* $150+.

h. Very small brass lamp with chimneyless burner. 1.5" wide at base, 2.125" tall to top of wick tube. Wick turner embossed with a ring of diamonds connected by a thin line. *Schwartz collection.* $65+.

i. Small brass finger lamp with chain held cap. Base incised with four horizontal lines. 2.25". *Cotting Collection.* $75+.

k. Gilded pot metal with girl and boy standing under light; celluloid shade with foreign burner. 4.75". *Baumgardner collection.* $200+.

l. Gilded gold urn style base with four feet. Embossed with design, milk glass shade. Wick riser marked "Night Lamp." 4.5" to top of shade. *Baumgardner collection.* $200+.

o. Silver plated finger lamp highly embossed with leaves and flowers. Removable lid and snuffer. Base marked "Meridan Silver Co. Reg. #086." 2.5". *Author's collection.* $100+.

m. Pewter base with embossed flowers and scrolls. Shade is threaded greenish Vaseline with opalescent on the inside. 6" to top of shade. Base has a name inscribed "Madeleine" on front. *Baumgardner collection.* $200+.

n. Brass cupid lamp balancing an urn on the head. Very small unmarked burner similar to those marked "Night Light." Missing small clear glass chimney . 5.5" to collar top. *Author's collection.* $100+.

p. Go-To-Bed lamp with heavy ornamental brass base. Applied handle has an indentation to hold a match. Holes around removable sleeve allow for air. Two thumb screws hold the cylindrical chimney with flared base. Pick-wick-style burner. 2" to top of burner. *Ruf collection.* $300+.

q. Small nickel plated traveling alcohol lamp. When closed, measures 1.75" wide, 2.5" tall, and 1" deep. When opened, shows match holder at top and removal font with screw-on cap attached by ball links. Bottom embossed "U. S. A. M.D. PIONEER NEW YORK, N.Y." Possibly used by a physician. *Schwartz collection.* $50+.

r. Tin "Kodak" dark room lamp with red and yellow lenses. 8". *Turner collection.* $75+.

Catalog Reprint of Foreign Burners

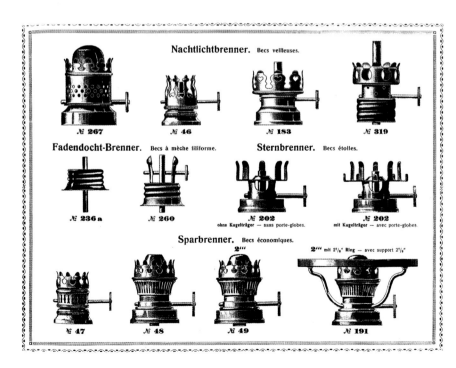

Catalog Reprints of European Lamps

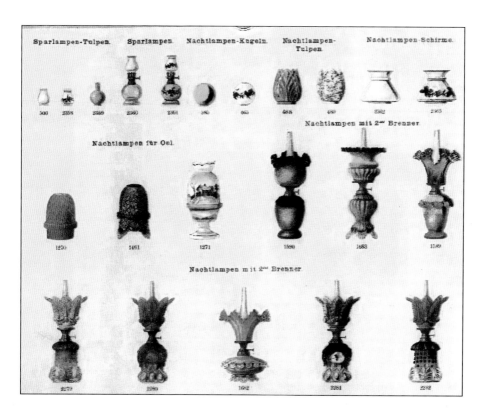

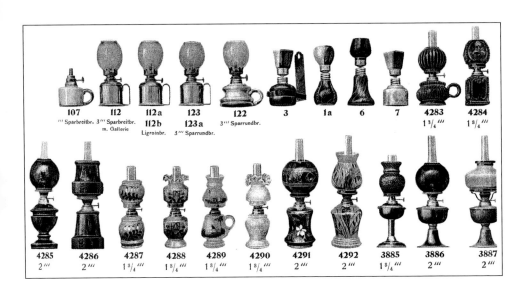

107	112	112a	123	122	3	1a	6	7	4283	4284
''' Sparbreitbr.	3''' Sparbreitbr. m. Gallerie	112b Ligroinbr.	123a 3''' Sparrundbr.	3''' Sparrundbr.					1 3/4 '''	1 3/4 '''

4285	4286	4287	4288	4289	4290	4291	4292	3885	3886	3887
2'''	2'''	1 3/4 '''	1 3/4 '''	1 3/4 '''	1 3/4 '''	2'''	2'''	1 3/4 '''	2'''	2'''

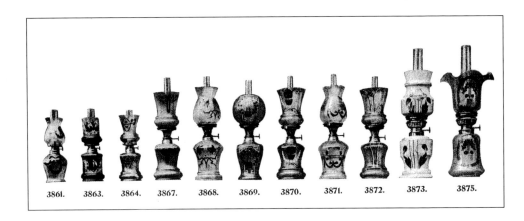

3861.	3863.	3864.	3867.	3868.	3869.	3870.	3871.	3872.	3873.	3875.

A Brief History of European Miniature Lamps

Author's note: Mr. Zbar has traveled extensively through Europe and is an active member of the Night Light Club here in the United States. As miniature oil lamp enthusiasts and collectors, we just cannot thank Mr. Zbar enough for providing us with copies of foreign miniature oil lamp manufactures and his extensive research.

A major issue for collectors, curators, and appraisers of relics from antiquity is authenticity and provenance. Who among us was there to see the item *in situ,* new on a shelf in a guild marketplace, country store or factory one hundred or one thousand years ago and on that basis can now vouch for the item as the real thing? Who can we trust *today* to speak with *absolute certainty* about the age and origin of antiques in general and miniature oil lamps in particular? It is an issue but certainly not beyond the reach of anyone willing to seek out and study the few important clues left to us through the ages.

My entry into the world of miniature oil lamps came from a glancing blow off my interest in Vaseline glass. One day while looking for glass in a second hand store in a northern European country, I found one of the finest lamps I would ever have the opportunity to own. It was a perfect opalescent Vaseline mini, but for the burner which was incomplete. The shade was sitting on the shelf next to the base, but (unbeknownst to me at the time) the fitter ring was missing. I bought the piece for a pittance and took it home knowing it was special, but I had no idea just how special it was! A year later I happened to see a miniature lamp book at an antique fair and saw my exact lamp pictured and at that moment realized what I had been missing. My year in the dark inspired me to seek the light so to speak. From then on, all of my antique buying trips to Europe included seeking out original catalogs and data on early oil lamp lamps as well as the lamps themselves. I came to know several "lamp people" throughout Europe. They are folks whose life missions are about the search for lamps, lamp parts, lamp books, and other lamp people. Serendipity has, therefore, led me to the clues which enabled me to learn a bit about these things that we so passionately seek and admire.

I don't know much, as I am just an observer and reporter. What little I do know concerns what was happening with oil lamps in a few countries in Europe from about 1880 to 1920. There is still a lot to learn, a lot of countries out there to visit, and a lot of lamp people to meet. Then I met the author, Marge Hulsebus. Marge honored me by asking that I share some of what I have learned so far with all of you by writing a short synopsis for this, her second book on miniature oil lamps. And it really is an honor and my pleasure to do this for my fellow lamp collectors, so here goes.

I have been fortunate to come across about fifteen sales catalogs for oil lamps and lamp parts from Germany, Denmark, and Sweden. The catalogs date from about 1891 to 1917. For brevity I have chosen the catalogs and pages which most clearly illustrate the widest style range of miniature lamps and parts and which cover the widest range of dates. Many of the catalogs I have are copies of copies, although some were copied by me from original catalogs that are over one hundred years old. Understandably, many of the inclusions herein are of poor reproduction quality. They are, however, of great historical importance and for that reason I hope that readers will bear with the poor image quality. A number of the lamps in these catalogs are lamps very familiar to most collectors. Although some of the painting styles vary, the forms are quite recognizable. Finally, the period covered, roughly thirty-five years from 1881-1917 clearly shows the progression in style from Victorian to Art Nouveau. This is most clearly represented in the design patterns expressed on the hand painted white milk glass lamps and Bristol glass lamp shades and bases. Period recognition is an important step in dating objects from antiquity.

Photo #1

The first catalog is from *Arvid Böhlmarks Lampfabrik, Stockholm, Sweden 1891-1892.* In photo **#1** Böhlmarks was a manufacturing and wholesale reseller active in Sweden from about 1872 through the early 20th century. Each year saw a new catalog, and the company made both lamps and parts for domestic and export markets. Their goods were sold through company stores, as well as through unaffiliated retail outlets.

Photo #2

In photo #2, note lamps numbered 361 and 109. These finger lamps are typical cobalt, clear, amber, and red in color, and were sold with white milk glass shades. Numbers 363 and 343 may be familiar, as brass lamp bases with painted white or green milk glass shades. All of the pieces offered for sale in this catalog are clearly Victorian in style and design.

The second catalog of interest is again *Arvid Böhlmarks, Stockholm, Sweden 1899*. Photo #3 shows a turn of the century catalog cover. Photo #4 pictured many of the same lamps, still Victorian in style and design, that were available from as early as 1891. However, note lamp number 347. This lamp is often found today in red, green, and blue, with hand painted white enamel paint, glossy base, and frosted shade. An example of the lamp is pictured in this book. Also note lamp number 344, 345, and 346 with the "notched" or saw-tooth edged shade. These lamps are also pictured in this book. Other lamps with ruffled shades in white milk glass are of typical, Victorian floral design.

Photo #3

Photo #4

The third catalog of interest is from *Ehrich & Graetz, Berlin, Germany 1905*. This catalog is interesting in that many burners, chimneys, shades, and miniatures are shown.

Most of the catalogs not only show the factory itself, but I often see photos of the interiors, including workers at each main station. The various burners available at the time are shown to include the Sternbrenner, common on smaller lamps and able to hold a chimney and shade and the famous Sparbrenner, with or without fitter ring. Floral designs, painted or embossed indicate a clear shift toward the Art Nouveau design movement, as evidenced by the smooth, flowing pattern of the flowers and leaves, quite different than the representations of the earlier, Victorian period. See photos #5, 6, and 7. It is important to note that the Art Nouveau movement came earlier to France, Germany, and England than to Northern Europe and the USA. Also, the Art Nouveau movement was called *Jurgend Stil* (or a similar spelling) in most of the Germanic and Scandinavian countries.

Gesamt-Ansicht des Fabrik-Etablissements im Jahre 1905.

Photo #5

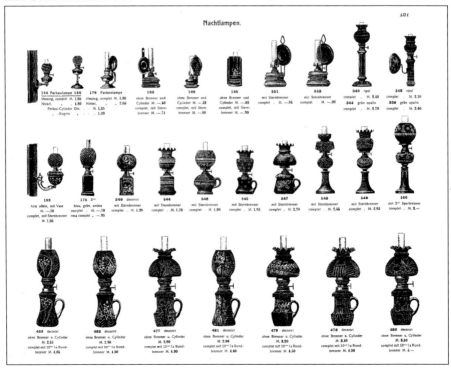

Photo #6

Photo #7

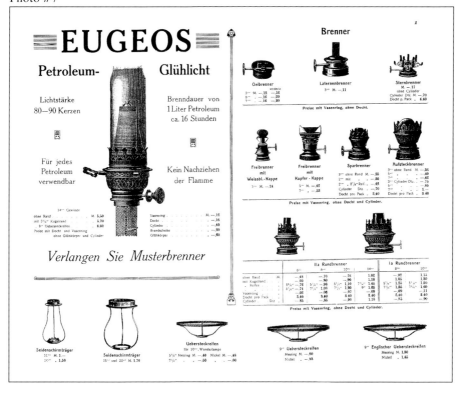

The fourth catalog of interest is from *Fyens Glasvaerk, Denmark, 1903.* These glass works were located on the Island of Fyn, the middle island of Denmark. Factories were in different cities on Fyn, however, Odense was perhaps one of the finest. The lamps of this time also reflect the designs of the times. See photos #8 and #9.

Photo #9

Photo #8

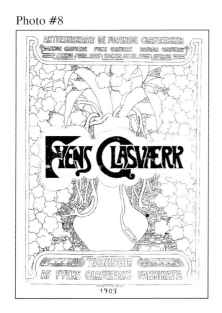

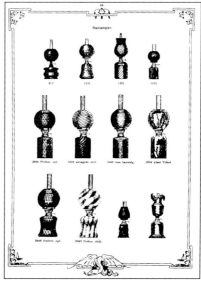

The fifth catalog of interest is *Fog & Morup, Copenhagen, Denmark 1913*. Fog & Morup were like Arvid Böhlmarks, in Sweden. They were wholesalers and manufacturers as well, and they sold products manufactured by Fyens Glasvaerk. Photo #10 shows the cover of the catalog and note the style of the font as it is clearly Art Nouveau. Photo #11 shows some of the shades available for "natlampekupler" (nitelampshades). Note that the styles fit the Sparbrenner burner. Photo #12 shows some of the "decorations of nitelamps" available. Number 466 is quite famous as is number 467. The style is late Art Nouveau, but still, the catalog offers standard lamps which are shown in other catalogs and reference books I have from Fyens Glasvaerk as early as 1903. Photos #13 and #14 show typical lamps that are familiar to us including Smith 480 and 481 along with painted white milk glass and bracket lamps.

Photo #11

Photo #10

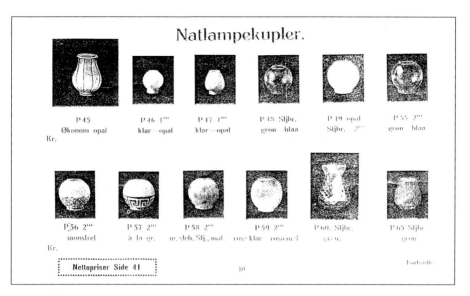

Photo #12

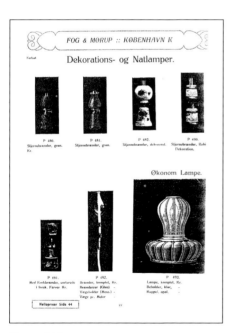

Photo #13

Photo #14

251

Finally, we have another catalog from *Arvid Böhlmarks Lampfabrik, Stockholm, Sweden 1917* shown in Photo #15. This catalog shows "goldmedals" from their sales efforts in Brussels, St. Petersburg, Antwerp, and Lubeck. Additionally, the catalog indicates that they are a sales agent for Pukebergs Glasbruk Nybro, Sweden. Pukeberg is famous in Sweden for its quality glass products, including many miniature oil lamps. I have done research from Pukebergs catalogs, and found many miniature lamps we have listed from Smith 1 and II, as well as Marge Hulsebus's first book. Photo #16 shows several lamps collectors have purchased from me. In particular, numbers 347, 348, 349, and 350 which was available in white, light green, dark green, and cobalt. These were produced by Pukeberg Glasbruk, and were available through 1917 in the original thin glass variety with the original Spar Brenner burner. I have found one variety with thicker glass, in wild colors such as orange, red, and cased glass and I have dated these remakes from 1920 through about 1970. The remakes were produced by Pukeberg from the original molds, and can be dated by the type of burner used. I believe, however, that the original Spar Brenner burner variety was no longer offered by about 1920. I have spoken to retired glass blowers who worked at Pukeberg, and who have corroborated this information for me. Number 347, glossy base and frosted shade is the same lamp that was shown in the catalog from Arvid Böhlmarks above, 1899, or offered for almost 20 years! Various other shades are shown as available at the time. As of yet I have found no catalogs showing miniature lamps from later than 1917.

In conclusion, I can only say the catalogs and photos speak for themselves. I am basically just a reporter, bringing you the information I have found from the corners of the European Continent. As indicated by the catalogs themselves, embossing and painting styles on the lamps followed typical styles of the times so that one can reasonably infer the age of a lamp in this way. Some painted lamps which were offered new for decades are more difficult to accurately date, but if they come to us with original, Spar Brenner burners, I feel that one can safely class them as highly collectible miniatures unlike more recent remakes. There are, however, hand painted miniatures which come to us with more recent burners which are not Spar Brenner burners and are not (in my opinion) to be placed in the same class as those with original Spar Brenner burners. As for the Pukeberg Glasbruk as well as other glass manufacturers of the high period, burners were imported from Germany and other countries and fitted on the lamp-glass blown in the various countries.

—Darrel Zbar

AKTIEBOLAGET

ARVID BÖHLMARKS LAMPFABRIK

KUNGL. HOFLEVERANTÖR

STOCKHOLM
ETABLERAD 1872

□ □ □

HUFVUDKONTOR OCH FABRIK: HÖGBERGSGATAN 19 OCH 21

BUTIKER:
NORRMALMSTORG 4 • STORA NYGATAN 33 • HÖGBERGSGATAN 19

ÄGARE AF PUKEBERGS GLASBRUK, NYBRO

FILIAL I MALMÖ: SÖDRA FÖRSTADSGATAN 2

GULDMEDALJER:

STOCKHOLM	1897	ANTWERPEN	1894
GEFLE	1901	LÜBECK	1895
HELSINGBORG	1903	MALMÖ	1896
NORRKÖPING	1906	BRÜSSEL	1897
	S:T PETERSBURG 1908		

CENTRALTRYCKERIET, STOCKHOLM 1917.

Photo #15

Photo #16

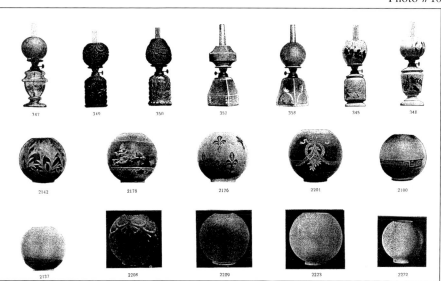

253

Reproduction of
Victorian Miniature Oil Lamps

Catalog images courtesy of B&P Lamp Supply, Inc.

Bibliography

Hulsebus, Marjorie. Victorian Miniature Lamps, 1996. Schiffer Publishing Ltd.; Atglen, PA.

McDonald, Ann Gilbert. Evolution of the Night Lamp, 1979. Wallace Homestead Book Co.: Des Moines, IA.

Ruf, Bob and Pat. Fairy Lamps, 1996. Schiffer Publishing Ltd.: Atglen, PA.

Smith, Frank R. and Ruth E. Miniature Lamps, 1978. Schiffer Publishing Ltd.: Atglen, PA.

Smith, Ruth. Miniature Lamps II, 1892. Schiffer Publishing Ltd.: Atglen, PA.

Thuro, Catherine M.V. Oil Lamps, 1976. Wallace Homestead Book Co.: Des Moines, IA.

Thuro, Catherine M.V. Oil Lamps II, 1983. Wallace Homestead Book Co.: Des Moines, IA.

US $49.95

9 780764 321047   5 4 9 9 5

ISBN: 0-7643-2104-8